THEOLOGIANS TODAY: HANS URS VON BALTHASAR

Other titles in the THEOLOGIANS TODAY series:

Yves M. J. Congar, OP
F. X. Durrwell, CSSR
Hans Küng
Henri de Lubac, SJ
Karl Rahner, SJ
Edward Schillebeeckx, OP
F. J. Sheed

THEOLOGIANS TODAY: a series selected and edited
by Martin Redfern

# HANS URS VON BALTHASAR

SHEED AND WARD · LONDON AND NEW YORK

First published 1972

Sheed & Ward Inc, 64 University Place, New York, N.Y. 10003
and Sheed & Ward Ltd, 33 Maiden Lane, London WC2E 7LA



Nihil obstat: John M. T. Barton, S.T.D., L.S.S.
Imprimatur: ✠ Victor Guazzelli, V.G
Westminster, 19 April, 1972

Library of Congress Catalog Number 72-2166

This book is set in 12/14 Monotype Imprint

Made and printed in Great Britain by
Billing & Sons Limited, Guildford and London

# CONTENTS

## Sources and Acknowledgments

"Scripture as the Word of God" (1949) is from *Selection I: A Yearbook of Contemporary Thought*, ed. Cecily Hastings and Donald Nicholl, London and New York, Sheed & Ward, 1953.

"Thérèse of Lisieux: the Church and the Contemplative Life" (1950) is from *Therese of Lisieux: The Story of a Mission*, London and New York, Sheed & Ward, 1953.

"The Perfectibility of Man" (1963) is from *A Theological Anthropology*, New York, Sheed & Ward, 1967; and *Man in History*, London, Sheed & Ward, 1968.

"The Last Five Stations of the Cross" (1964) is from *The Way of the Cross*, London, Burns & Oates/Sheed & Ward, 1969; and New York, Herder & Herder, 1969.

# INTRODUCTION

The last twenty-five years, and in particular the last ten years, have seen a remarkable flowering of Roman Catholic theology. But for the non-specialist—for the busy parish priest, the active layman, the student—the very wealth of this development presents a range of problems. With which theologian does he begin? Which theologians will he find the most rewarding? Can he ignore any of them?

There are no quick or final answers to such questions, of course, but I hope that this new *Theologians Today* series will help many Catholics to find their own answers more easily. It is designed to achieve two main purposes. Each individual book provides a short but representative introduction to the thought of an outstanding Catholic theologian of the present day, and the series as a whole demonstrates the kind of relationship existing between the best contemporary Catholic theology and official Church teaching.

Both purposes are met by the framework common to all the books. For each book I have selected—and arranged in order of original publication—four pieces which indicate the range in time, approach, and special interest of the theologian concerned. Partly to make my selections more 'objective', but mainly to emphasise the close connection between the theologian's writing and the teaching of Vatican II, I have keyed the articles to the four major documents of that Council—the four Constitutions, on the Church, on Revelation, on the Liturgy, and on the Church in the Modern World.

The selections are very much my own. The theologians themselves, or other editors, would doubtless have made different choices. Nevertheless, I feel that—granted my self-imposed limitations of space and conciliar theme, and the further necessary limitations imposed by copyright or by a proper preference for the out-of-print or inaccessible over the widely available—I have done my own best for men to whom I owe a large debt of gratitude.

The poem-meditations on the Crucifixion which conclude this selection may come as a surprise, but they are appropriate. There is a literary quality about Hans Urs von Balthasar's approach to theology, an openness to the artistic and mystical as well as the rational in man, that is refreshing. This quality characterizes all the the first three articles, especially perhaps those on the ecclesial nature of St Thérèse's contemplative life and on man's perfectibility.

MARTIN REDFERN

# 1. Scripture as the Word of God

"By revelation the deepest truth about God and the salvation of man is made clear to us in Christ, who is the Mediator and at the same time the fullness of all revelation."—*Dogmatic Constitution on Divine Revelation*, I, 2.

Scripture is the Word of God witnessing to the Word of God. The one Word, therefore, appears both as the witnessing Word and as the Word which is witnessed to, as if they each sprang from the other. The *Word to which witness is given* is essentially Jesus Christ, the eternal Word of the Father who took it upon himself to become flesh so as to bear witness in the flesh to the truth and life of God; he manifests this life because he *is* God. This manifestation of the Word constitutes the focal point in the whole economy of salvation. It reaches into the future, beyond the Apostles and Church history right into the last days, and stretches backwards through God's revelation of the Word in the Old Testament, beyond the law and the prophets into the very beginning of Creation. For God rests all creation upon his Word (Heb 1:3) and it is all accomplished through the Word, for the Word and in the Word; he stands at the head of all, and in him all subsist (Col 1:16–17); for, since he is the Son of Man as well as the Logos of God, he is the first and the last (Rev 1:17). The *witnessing Word* has its own distinctive function;

it is the series of Scriptures which accompany, and, as it were, mirror, the progressive revelation of the Word in the flesh. The revealed Word is the Word in the mode of action; God is grasped in his act of self-communication. The scriptural Word is the Word in the mode of contemplation: it contemplates its own action whilst simultaneously recording it. In order that this record should be perfectly valid and complete it has to be made by the Word itself, since only God can measure the scope of his revelation and grant to it the Word-form which it requires. The revealed Word is primarily the Son, who speaks of the Father through the Holy Spirit. The scriptural Word is primarily an operation of the Holy Spirit who, as the Spirit of the Father, prepares, accompanies, illumines and interprets the Son's Incarnation, and who, as Spirit of the Son, presents the Son's self-interpretation in a permanent, unchangeable form.

At first sight, then, it would seem as though there are two Words moving parallel to each other throughout sacred history. But this would be an illusion. Ultimately there is but one Word which bears witness to itself in the one revelation, as the following considerations hope to show.

1. Undoubtedly there are passages of Scripture which seem to point to a separation between the two forms of the Word. In the Gospels, for instance, our Lord speaks and lives, acts and suffers without making any attempt to have everything set down in writing. The documentation is done only later,

by eye-witnesses writing under the direction of the Holy Spirit, which is already the Spirit of the Church; and yet all the time the person who has been listening most attentively to the Word is the Holy Spirit, who sets down what he has heard in the form that is most suitable to the Church. The same may be said about the Acts, the history of the Apostles, as about all the historical books of the Old Testament, although the differentiation becomes less marked in the Apocalypse and in the prophets. Admittedly, in the latter case, the Word comes first of all personally to the prophets as a "private revelation that is later made public"; but even here it is not quite certain whether this must happen orally before it is written down or whether it was put into written form from the very beginning. Revelation *to* the prophets and promulgation *through* the prophets are so intimately connected that they almost constitute a single act of revelation which is performed by the Spirit with a view to the future—or past—Incarnation of the Son. The two become merged into one in those cases where there is no reason to assume that revelation took place before it was written down, as in the Wisdom Books. Here revelation occurs in the very moment that it is written down by the inspired author. Of the Apostles' letters the same is true. Even if a certain gap is discernible in the seven letters of the Apocalypse—it is to the Apostle John that the Spirit first of all dictates the letters to the congregation, after which the Apostle writes them down—this gap cannot be found in the usual letters of the Apostles. However, one should not overlook the interpretative, quasi-contemplative character of the Wisdom Books and the letters of the Apostles. Just as the first interpret Jewish sacred history and laws for the sake of the chosen people, so the letters interpret the Gospels for the sake of the Church. Consequently the transition from the witnessing Word to the Word of which witness is given takes place smoothly, and their clear separation is transformed into practical identity. Revelation, therefore, occurs partly before the Scripture, and partly in Scripture. In other words, Scripture has its part in God's self-revelation in Christ through the Spirit.

2. The second consideration takes us deeper still and finally discredits the notion that there is only a parallel between the witnessing Word and the Word to which it bears witness. The central Word spoken by God, which gathers into itself all the manifold aspects of God's Word and represents the consummation of them all, is Jesus Christ, the Incarnate God. But he appeared under the sign of obedience in order to fulfil everything that was demanded by the Father, in order to redeem and justify Creation. He does this by allowing his earthly existence as the Word-made-flesh to be moulded at each and every moment by all the forms of the Word which are already present in the law and the prophets. He lives in order that the Scripture might be fulfilled. Thus he assimilates the scriptural Word into his own life and allows it to live concretely and utterly

in him, in the flesh. During the course of his life both movements become evident: more and more the Word becomes flesh by transforming the abstract law and the prophetical promises into the concrete, divine presence, whilst the flesh becomes more and more identified with the Word as Christ unites the scriptural Word ever more intimately with his own person, and makes his earthly existence a complete expression of all God's previous revelations. He is the living commentary, the ultimate interpretation, the interpretation intended from the beginning. Not only does he fulfil every Word of the Father (the vertical Word from above); he also fulfils every word ordained towards him from history and tradition (the horizontal Word). But if, on the one hand, he is its complete fulfilment because he is the person who was ultimately to come, he is no less its living and progressive fulfilment. The fact that he is both these things, that he also remains both, opens up the possibility that there will be Scripture consequent upon his life, though of an altogether different kind. The law and the prophets were the formal guarantee of the Word which was one day to be made man; they were God's Word in human characters; furthermore they were an adequate expression of revelation and not something relative which would later need to be revised. Clearly, then, the Word of the Old Testament marks the point at which God introduced his mediation, the place where he brought himself closest to man, the form under which he made himself available to man. As one can see from the whole of Psalm 118 the role which the law used to play in man's life at that time prefigures the role of the Eucharist in the New Testament. The fact that there was still to be Scripture even after Christ had gathered into himself the whole of Scripture, and realized its promise of eternal life (John 5:39–40), only goes to show that by fulfilling he does not destroy. It is the way of man to bring things to a close when he fulfils them, but when the Father fulfils his promises he neither destroys them nor brings them to a close but reveals new promises, thus remaining what he always was—he who fulfils all expectations beyond expectation. Even in the flesh our Lord remains what he always is, the Word. He does not dissociate himself from what has been said of him previously, nor from what he himself has said or what has been reported of him. The Gospel is his living teaching preserved for the Church in Scripture; but it is a new "incarnate" Scripture since (as the Fathers always insist) it partakes of his Incarnation and so constantly shares in his living inspiration. Every word which our Incarnate Lord utters is already inspired by the Holy Spirit, but so is the written word. The inspired Word does not lose its inspiration, as if inspiration had happened once and could now be forgotten; on the contrary, this inspiration remains with it always and is a feature of it for all time, infusing it with that quality of vitality by which our Lord shows that he is not imprisoned in the letter; he is to be received as the Spirit, which always remains more vital, more powerful and greater than the letter. Therefore, whilst the Incarnate Lord on the one hand absorbs the Scripture into himself to raise it to its proper perfection as the Word of God the Father in the Son, on the other hand he lets it proceed from him to raise it to its proper perfection as the Word of the Spirit, which he sends forth at the end of his life on earth when returning to the Father. In neither form can Scripture be treated as a witnessing Word separable from the Word to which it bears witness, for it is the one Word of God united in the Incarnation.

Set into this context the Fathers' dictum that Scripture is the Body of the Logos can be better appreciated. If this dictum is not to be regarded as a mere phantasy or metaphor it has to be applied to the whole process of the Incarnation. One may speak of Christ's Body in several ways. The fundamental form of Christ's Body—the basis of all other forms—is the historical Body which he received from Mary, in which he lived on earth and which he took to heaven at his ascension. The ultimate form towards which the Incarnation is directed is the mystical (though no less real) Body, i.e., the Church. In the Church men are united to his historical Body, through which they share in the life of Christ and of God. But in order that no one should think of the historical Body and the mystical Body as two disparate units there are two mediating forms which enable one to make the transition from the historical to the mystical Body; these are *the Eucharist* and *the Scriptures.* They bring the Incarnate Logos to the faithful; in them the Logos, who is the beginning and the end, also becomes the way (*via*), the Eucharist in so far as it is the divine life (*vita*), and the Scriptures in so far as they are the divine Word and the divine Truth (*veritas*). The Eucharist affords the marvellous possibility of freeing Christ's historical Body from the limitations of space and time, mysteriously multiplying its Presence. Without any loss of unity it provides every Christian with his necessary and indispensable nourishment (John 6:53–8), making each of them a member of Christ, knitting them all into one Body which pulses with divine life. It is through the Eucharist that the Church comes to life as the Body of Christ, for the distribution of our Lord's Body to so many people means that all these divided men are made one in him. "Is not the bread that we break a participation in Christ's Body? The one bread makes us one Body" (1 Cor 10:16–17). The same marvellous suspension of space and time marks the manner in which the Scriptures contain our Lord as Word and as Spirit—and once more neither his unity nor his concreteness is impaired. The Word does not cease to be a unique, concrete presence in the Scriptures any more than Christ's Body ceases to be the one historical Body because it is made available in the Eucharist. Both mediating forms have this in common: they universalize Christ's Body without impairing its concreteness.

Nevertheless this universal validity of the scriptural Word has nothing whatsoever to do with the kind of abstract universality which human generalizations are based on. The scriptural Word makes the Incarnate Lord present in a way analogous to the way in which his historical Body is made present in the Eucharist, and Origen exhorts Christians to cultivate the same reverent attitude toward the scriptural Word as they adopt towards the Body of Christ in the Eucharist. In the same tradition the author of the *Imitation of Christ* says, "For in this life I find there are two things most necessary for me, without which this miserable life would be unsupportable; for the Word of God is the light of my soul, and thy Sacrament is the bread of my soul. These also may be called the two tables set on either side in the storehouse of thy holy Church. One is the table of the Holy Altar, having the holy bread—that is the precious Body of Christ. The other is that of the divine law, containing holy doctrine, teaching the right faith and leading most securely even to the interior of the veil, where is the Holy of Holies" (Bk. IV, ch. xi). "Next to the Body and Blood of our Lord there is nothing which the Catholic Church holds so high and sacred as the Word of God in the sacred Scriptures,", as J. B. Heinrich wrote nearly a century ago (1881). It is the historical Christ and his Body, the Church, which make both of them possible; they are unconditional, exclusive gifts from the Bridegroom to his Bride, beyond the reach, capacity and enjoyment of all outsiders. We learn that many of the martyrs died rather than hand over the sacred Scriptures to the heathen, just as Tarsisius died in order to prevent them stealing the Eucharist. In both cases the Spirit is co-operating in the work of the Son: the miraculous change in the elements is attributable to the Spirit, and so is the formation of the Word into Scripture. For it is the function of the Spirit to mould the mystical Body of Christ by universalizing the historical Christ. The fact that the Scriptures do not contain the Word in a sacramental mode in no way weakens the force of the analogy. For just as our Lord in the sacrament is ever ready to surrender himself to those who receive him with burning faith, similarly he is ready to give himself personally, as the Word and the Truth, to everyone who approaches the Scriptures prayerfully and in search of the Truth. They also receive the divine Word. *Per evangelica dicta deleantur nostra delicta.*

When we look at it from this angle, the connection between *Scripture* and *Tradition* can easily be seen. The scriptural Word is a gift of the Bridegroom to his Bride. It is meant for the Church and so can be said to belong to the Church: but the Word of God is head of the Church and therefore stands out above the Church. This shifting relationship which allows the Church the disposal of the Scriptures—but only insofar as it allows itself to be disposed of by God's Word—must be discussed in terms of the relationship between Bride and Bridegroom, which is a mystery of divine love. God took to himself a human form, even going so far as to hand over his power to the Church so that the Church might be enriched and lifted up; this is the degree to which the Church in its turn must humble itself, to serve as a handmaid and to realize that the Son's greatest glory lay in humbling himself. When the Church maintains that Tradition as well as Scripture constitutes a source of faith it is completely false to suggest that it is trying to escape from the authority of Scripture by appealing to ill-founded traditions of its own devising. The truth is that since the Incarnation the letter of Scripture must be an instrument in the service of Christ's living Body, whose actions can never be restricted to the mere letter. The Scriptures themselves assure us that this is so. "There are many other miracles Jesus did in the presence of his disciples which are not written down in this book. There is much else besides that Jesus did; if all of it were put in writing, I do not think the world itself would contain the books which would have to be written" (John 20:30; 21:25). The witnessing Word assures us that the Word to which it bears witness, the revealed Word, is so infinitely rich that written words are incapable of describing it. This marks the essential difference between the Word since the Incarnation and the Word previous to the Incarnation. In the Old Testament the Word, in one sense, had still to come; since it had not been completely realized and fulfilled it could not be the subject of tradition—it could not be handed on (in the sense that Tradition is a sign of how the Word, when it is fully manifest, breaks through the framework of the written word). Since, moreover, the Word took the shape of law and prophecy, human speech and writing was capable of representing it adequately—although here, too, it was presupposed that the Word could only be received by someone standing in the grace of the same Spirit who had spoken the Word. But there was no obligation for the Jews to believe that God had made any other revelation to Abraham and Moses, or had spoken any other words to the prophets, except those recorded in Scripture either at the time or subsequently. During the Old Dispensation, Tradition did not serve as a source of faith, and the warrant of Scripture enjoyed the same validity as Protestantism later accorded to it in regard to the New Testament. After the Incarnation Tradition had to be a source of faith. However, it would be an error to deduce this truth from the fact that all history is organic. It is not the organic character of history but the uniqueness of the person of Christ, the God–Man, and his connection with his mystical Body, the Church, which accounts for it. Without Tradition even the Scriptures of the New Testament would still retain the essential features of the Old; they would still be laws and prophecies; they would not be the Word and Body of a Person who continues to dwell in his Church as a living Eucharistic Body (something which did not exist in the Old Testament). This explains why strict Protestantism, once it has denied the Mass and transubstantiation, then proceeds, quite logically, to assume an extreme eschatological attitude. The God of the Old Testament delivers his clearcut messages from the heavens; he does not deliver himself to his people. Christ, on the contrary, does give himself over to the Church, because it was for the Church that he gave himself on the Cross (Eph 5:2, 25), because the Father gave him over to us on the Cross (Rom 8:32) because, finally, he gave up his Spirit on the Cross (John 19:30), the same which he breathed into his Church on Easter Day (John 20:22). Thus he gives himself to his Church in the Eucharist and in the Scriptures, but each of these bodily forms is a means of making the Church a unique life, unchanging yet infinitely various. Since, however, the witnessing Word is incapable of containing the infinite richness of the revealed Word, it means that there is always an overflow, which the Church receives as the vital, Eucharistic, presence of Christ. This vital presence itself is then reflected back in the form of the Word which is the principle of Tradition. Even the Scriptures are a Tradition insofar as they are one of the forms in which Christ gave himself to the Church, and in this sense Tradition existed before the Scriptures, because, without Tradition, the authority of the Scriptures themselves could never have been established. At the same time Scripture acts as a guarantee for all subsequent Tradition since it is God's mirror of God's revelation; without this guarantee it would be just as impossible for the Church to spread the truth as it would be impossible for the Church to be holy without the Eucharist.

The scriptural Word is God's Word witnessing to itself, which it does in three ways. It is the Word of God, it is what God says *about* the world and what he says *to* mankind.

1. *The Word of God.* Word—not vision, nor feeling and not simply the kind of stammering to which men are reduced whenever they begin to talk about God. It is an inimitably clear Word, quite plain and definite. Its character as a Word is rooted in the twofold mystery of the Trinity and the Incarnation. Because God has within himself the eternal Word which eternally expresses him, he is eminently expressible; and because this same Word has taken human form and, in human words and deeds, expresses what God *is*, it can be understood by men. The first without the second would be of no help to us, whilst the second without the first would be inconceivable. What makes it possible for Christ to translate heavenly truth into an adequate earthly form is the fact that he unites in his person both divine and human nature. "Believe me, we speak of what is known to us and testify of what our eyes have seen . . . but one who comes from heaven must needs be beyond the reach of all: he bears witness of things he has seen and heard" (John 3:11, 31–2). And yet, because God's truth is essentially personal (the Word being the person of the Son), it is also a sovereign and free truth. The

Son is not a mechanical photograph of the Father but is that return of love to the Father which can only be made by one who enjoys complete sovereignty. Hence the translation of the divine Word into the human Word is the Son's act of sovereign freedom and has no guarantee outside the Son himself. "I am the Truth." "No one comes to the Father except through me." If the Word is to be received, therefore, faith is necessary for two reasons. In the first place, because the truth which is being communicated is divine and surpasses the capacity of the human reason. Secondly, because the truth is personal and can only be received through trusting in the free act of the divine person who presents it, for the disparity between the content of divine truth and the human form in which it is expressed cannot be overcome except in the person of the Word Incarnate. The Incarnation, in fact, is the event which removes this disparity. In other words, the relation between the human and divine element in Scripture falls into the same pattern as the relation between human and divine nature in Christ. Christ's human nature is entirely a medium for expressing (*principium quo*) his divine person (*principium quod*), which in its turn is the expression of the Father; similarly each word of Scripture is genuinely human but is entirely a means of expressing a divine content. Consequently the much-discussed problem of the relation between the "literal sense"and the "spiritual sense" of Scripture is actually a Christological problem and must be solved by recognizing that the "two" senses are related in the same way as human and divine nature are related in Christ. The human element represents an immediately available medium for approaching divine revelation; it is a veil through which divine truth can be perceived even though it will not be completely transparent until the Resurrection; it is so much part of God's plan that it will not be removed or dispensed with in eternity. The spiritual sense has not to be sought "behind" the letter, but in the letter, just as the Father is not discovered "behind" the Son but in him and through him. To stop at the literal sense and ignore the spiritual sense would be to treat the Son as nothing more than a man, and would involve us in the unbelief of the Jews. Everything human in Christ is a revelation of God and refers to God; his whole life, his work, his sufferings and his Resurrection all express and interpret God in human terms.

The fact that the Son does adequately express the content of divine truth in human form in no way affects the truth that the content, which is God himself, must always be greater than the form in which it is expressed. One has no more chance of understanding the divine meaning of Scripture if one rests content with the letter than one has of believing in the divinity of Christ whilst refusing to look beyond his human nature. Such understanding is only granted when one waits for it in faith, which means being ready to keep on listening and not demanding a complete vision of what is hearing; it is granted in an open and infinite progression whose sole measure is the operation of the Holy Spirit (Rom 12:3; Eph 4:7). Faith is the principle of all understanding which opens up the creature's consciousness so that the can participate in the divine consciousness, and it gives him access to the divine meaning of the Word from within, through a sort of intimacy with God (1 Cor 2:9–16); therefore the person who will receive the gift of understanding in the greatest measure will be the saint, who opens himself most completely to the Holy Spirit and puts himself at the Spirit's disposition. The saint avoids a failing which most men, under the weight of original sin, seem to commit automatically and with desperate obstinacy; that is, they try to impose human limits upon the meaning of God's Word. They acknowledge its truth, but only so long as it suits their human modes of thought and their everyday conventions, so long as it does not disturb them and allows them to treat some accepted meaning as final—so long as they can do what Mary Magdalen was told not to do: "Do not cling to me thus; I have not yet gone up to my Father's side" (John 20:17). If we claim that any Scriptural text has been finally understood and its meaning completely exhausted we are actually denying that Scripture is the Word of God and is inspired. Nor should we take freedom from error to be the main effect of inspiration in Scripture (there are many books free from error which are not inspired). Our attention should be directed towards those permanent qualities in it which show that the Holy Spirit as *auctor primarius* is present in each word of Scripture, ever ready to guide men into the depths of divine truth so long as they are sincerely trying to understand this Word, which is his Word. The primary content of Scripture, always, is God. Whether describing the world and its history, whether proclaiming laws or telling parables, it is God who is speaking and it is about himself that he is speaking. He is speaking about himself and his judgement on the world. By penetrating into the Spirit of Scripture we are introduced to God's inner life, learning to make his judgements about the world into our own.

2. Therefore the Scripture, being the Word of God, is also *God's Word about the World*; once more, because it is inseparable from the revealed Word, the Son Incarnate. God has grounded the meaning of the world in the Son and will not have us seek it anywhere else. In him the world was created. To understand the phrase "in the beginning" of Creation (Gen 1:1) one has to remember that "the Word" is already there in this "beginning" (John 1:1). He provides the meaning and purpose of our lives, i.e., of believers first of all (Eph 11:4), but then, of "everything" (1 Tim 4:10), of "everything in heaven and on earth"; everything in creation has been planned, chosen and knit together so that the key to everything is found in him, who is "the first and the last" (Rev 1:17). And this is true not only because he is the Logos but also because of his Incarnation and Crucifixion. God did not prepare and lay the foundation of the world without foreseeing sin, without decreeing that the world should also be redeemed by the future Incarnation of his only-begotten Son.

The Redemption did not come into God's mind for the first time after the Creation of the world. Far from it. He created the world knowing that it would need redemption and would be the stage for the Redemption. From the very beginning this world was conceived and created by God not only *through* the Eternal Word but rather *for* it—for the Word which was to become flesh, which became flesh and dwelt amongst us. The world was created for Christ and Christianity. But if all creation is conceived through the Son and for the Son, then all creation shares in his formal character as the Word. As the Incarnate Word the Son is the supreme law of the world. Once this truth is recognized, God's Word can be seen to flow backwards over time so that the Incarnation is foreshadowed and provided for in the law and the prophecies, those forms of the Word which God had fixed for his dealings with mankind; it even stretches beyond the Old Testament, since the "nature" of every creature has had a form of the Word impressed upon it by the very fact of Creation, and there is a form graven on the hearts of the heathen which makes up for their lack of law and prophecy (Rom. 2:14–15). Looking at it from this centre of vision one can see that the existence of the heathens, as well as of the Jews, is controlled and nurtured by the Word of God. Simply being a man means being called by God into the Word, being made in the image of God, able to understand and answer his Word. Accordingly Alexandrine theology traces the rationality of all creatures back to the presence of the Logos in them (a view which allows equally for the *raison d'etre* of the sub-human creation). Summing up his opinion on this matter, St Maximus the Confessor said that there were three levels at which the Word was realized in the world: the Word as nature, the Word as Scripture, and the Word as the flesh in Christ. If we admit that the laws of nature and history must ultimately be measured by the law of Christ it follows that man has to listen to the Word of God in Christ, and to make his existential response to this Word, before he can discover the word which expresses his own self and "delivers" him. However much this human word may appear to be an expression of culture, art, philosophy, education or technics—of this world—it will in fact be an answer to the call of God, bringing man and the world back into God. By replying to God's Word man will become capable of "releasing" the Word which is dormant in natural things, announcing the message which everything has in it (Claudel), bringing to light the lower creation even as Christ has brought him to the light. But, as he makes this ascent, the nearer he comes to its peak, which is Christ, the more keenly he must sense the immediacy and actuality of the Word. In nature the Word is generalized, in history its uniqueness is unmistakable, whilst in revelation it displays a uniqueness which puts it outside the compass of the laws either of time or of history. In a flash God reveals his uniqueness and actuality in the "one man, Jesus Christ" (1 Tim 2:5), "eternally-now" (2 Cor 6:2; Heb 4:7).

3. Scripture is *God's message to man.* The word to which Scripture bears witness is not past but present—because eternal—not addressed to some other person but to me, now. Just as the Eucharist is not the commemoration of a past event but the "presenting" of the unique, eternal Body and sacrifice of our Lord, similarly Scripture is not just history but the channel by which God is for ever bringing his Word to us. If human existence at its deepest level is a dialogue with God, but one in which God's word to men is infinitely more important than man's word to God; if man can only give a correct answer when he is listening all the time for the Word (contemplation perhaps would express better what is meant); if, moreover, God has said once and for ever in Christ (Heb 1:1) what he has to say to every man, then reading the Scriptures and meditating upon them must be the surest way for me to discover quite concretely what God wants of me and intends for me. Here God has spoken; here he never ceases to express himself completely in his Word. This is the source to which the Church's preachers must go in order to be filled with the knowledge which they have to transmit to the faithful, but it is also the place to which every believer must go to encounter the Word of God personally and immediately. Every Word proceeding from the mouth of God, as our Lord says, is food for the soul. Aquinas interprets this a follows. "Whoever does not live by the Word of God has no life in him. For as the human body cannot live without earthly nourishment neither can the soul live without the

Word of God. But the Word proceeds from the mouth of God when he reveals his will through the testimony of the Scriptures" (*Cat. aurea in Matt.* 4:4). And the scriptural Word says more about God than any other word; it is christological in form, opening the way to God and leading us to him. If we may use such an expression, the Word is chosen by the Holy Spirit with such consummate art that it is perfectly definite without its thereby being limited or restricted (a limitation which cannot be avoided in human definitions and pronouncements); and not a single one of the truths which it propounds blocks one's view of other truths, whether these are immediately connected with it or seem difficult to reconcile with it. Far from being exclusive it opens up the truth at every point. This is a quality of Scripture which even the Church's definitions do not possess, because, although the definitions are preserved from error through the assistance of the Holy Spirit, they usually represent the close of a time of uncertainty; they allay doubts but do not open up new horizons. Scheeben is right when he says: "If we carefully search through Holy Scripture, meditating upon the different sayings and comparing various expressions and their meanings, we gain a much broader and richer understanding of revealed truth than that which is presented in the public, dogmatic teaching of the Church." However necessary such definitions may be for the Church's work, they are not the Christian soul's main source of nourishment.

If divine truth is imparted to souls through Christ

in the Scriptures, then, however inward or mystical the soul's conversation with God may be, it can never by-pass the Scriptures. This explains why the Protestants are so far from the mark when they attempt to play off the prophetical against the mystical side of Scripture (e.g. Heiler) or to set up the Word against mysticism (e.g., Brunner). Such an antithesis leaves us but two courses: either we fall back into the Old Testament conception of the Word, which disregards the soul's need of nourishment and ignores the foreshadowing of the Eucharist, or else we completely misunderstand Christian mysticism, which can have no standard other than the form of revelation contained in Scripture itself. Nor do we describe Scripture as mystical simply because it is inspired; in fact, the whole content of revelation in both the Old and New Testaments is nothing but a series of mystical experiences enjoyed by patriarchs, prophets, kings, apostles and disciples. And it is here that Christian mysticism should always find its canon, instead of being led away into the superficialities of individualistic psychology. Christian mysticism is scriptural mysticism; it means coming into contact with the Word in a particularly charismatic form since it is either directly or indirectly a revelation of the Word to the Church; it is essentially social. The Spirit remains with the Church, continuing to inspire Scripture throughout all centuries, eternally interpreting the revealed Word and "guiding the Church ever deeper into the truth" (John 16:13); the same Spirit which was at work in the Old Testament prophets is still at work in the "prophets" of the new dispensation whom Paul cites along with the Apostles as pillars of the Church (Eph 2:20; 3:5; 4:11). The reason why their writings are not accounted as "Holy Scripture" in the same way as the Bible arises from the fact that divine revelation was completed with our Lord and his eyewitnesses, and therefore the Scripture was fulfilled. But to speak of revelation coming to a "close" is extremely misleading. The fulfilment in question does not indicate an end so much as a beginning. It is Christ's fullness constantly unfolding into the fullness of the Church, the growth of both the Church and the world into the fullness of Christ and of God—as it is described in the letter to the Ephesians. Now the richness of Scripture begins to pour itself out into the Church, a richness such that the whole of time could never exhaust it. All human books have a limited content. One reads them, studies them and learns them by heart until the day comes when one has no more need of them. But Scripture is God's Word, and the further one penetrates into it the more it opens one s mind to the immensity of God. "May you and all the saints be enabled to measure in all its breadth and length and height and depth"—the four-dimensional space of divine truth! —"the love of Christ, to know what passes knowledge. May you be filled with all the completion God has to give" (Eph 3:18–19).

# 2. Thérèse of Lisieux: the Church and the Contemplative Life

"By the charity to which they lead, the evangelical counsels join their followers to the Church and its mystery in a special way. Because of this, the spiritual life of these followers should be devoted to the good of the whole Church. Thence arises their duty of working to implant and strengthen the kingdom of Christ in souls and to extend that kingdom to every land. This duty is to be discharged to the extent of their capacities and in keeping with the form of their proper vocation. The chosen means may be prayer or active undertakings."—*Dogmatic Constitution on the Church*, VI, 44.

Thérèse of Lisieux was directly entrusted by God with a mission to the Church. The very first sentence of Pius XI's speech at her beatification expressly refers to it: "The voice of God and the voice of his people have joined in extolling the Venerable Thérèse of the Child Jesus. The voice of God first made itself heard, and the faithful, recognizing the divine call, added their voices to the anthem of praise. We repeat, the voice of God was the first to speak." One may even say that Thérèse and the Curé d'Ars were the only two perfectly evident instances during the nineteenth century of a primarily theological mission. Catherine Labouré and Bernadette were both entrusted with a more restricted task, whilst Don Bosco and Gemma Galgani do not quite achieve the fullness of a primarily theological mission. And as no other instances have occurred since, the judgement of the faithful agrees with the saying of Pius XI, that Thérèse is the greatest saint of modern times.

Thérèse's mission, at the very first glance, displays the marks of a clearly defined, and quite exceptional character. This is much less due to the personal drama of the little saint than to the sacred form into which the trickling grains of petty anecdotes are compressed, into a hard, unbreakable block, by a firm invisible hand. It is contrary to all expectation that the simple, modest story of this little girl should eventually culminate, as it irrefutably does, in the enunciation of theological truths. Originally she herself never dreamt that she might be chosen to bear some fundamental message to the Church. She only became aware of it gradually; in fact, it did not occur to her until her task was almost completed, after she had already lived out her teaching and was writing the last chapters of her book. Suddenly, as she saw it all laid out before her, she recognized its strangeness, that in her obedience she had unwillingly conceived something beyond her own personality. And now that she saw it she also understood it, and seized it with a kind of violence. Ever since her childhood Thérèse had shown a striking inclination to meditating and reflecting upon herself. Which meant that when she discovered her mission she became intensely conscious of it in a manner rare amongst the saints. At that moment she realized she was to be set on a pedestal, and that every bit of her life, even its smallest details, would be used as a pattern for many of the "little ones". She scrutinizes her relationship to others who also had great missions, and aligns her own mission with that of Joan of Arc. "In my mission, as in Joan of Arc's, the will of God will triumph, despite the envy of men." She defines the content of her message ever more exactly, searching for more and more compact formulae for her doctrine of the little way. She regards the publication of her manuscript as "an important work"; she knows "that all the world will love me", and that her writings "will do a great deal of good". During her last months, as if making her last will and testament, she repeats constantly: "One must tell souls . . ." Exactly the same expressions recur in reference to the mission she is soon to begin in heaven: "I feel that my mission will soon begin—to teach souls to love God as I love him, to give them my 'little way'. If my wishes are realized, I shall spend my heaven on earth until the end of the world." And when her sister Pauline asked her what this little way was into which souls must be led, she answered with the deepest sense of her responsibility: "It is the way of spiritual childhood, the way of trust and total surrender. I will bring to them the little means which have served me so perfectly . . ."

Similarly she recognizes the function within the Church of her mission. She not only foresees the proclamation of her own sanctity—she was always aware of being "a saint" and never pretended otherwise, as is shown in her distributing her own relics, or at least not objecting to their distribution, as she lay on her death-bed; crucifix, pictures, rose-petals, even her hair, nails, tears and eyelashes. But she also, as it were, foresaw the canonization of her doctrine. The two are not separable—it is not so much her writings as her life itself which is her doctrine, especially since her writings speak about her life more than anything else. Nor does she hesitate to propose her life as an example for the Church, because it is in her life that she sees the realization of that doctrine which "can do much so good". She is to be counted as one of those who, in the phrase of Marie-Antoinette de Geuser, are "expropriated to serve the public use". So her life only contains exemplary value for the Church insofar as the Holy Spirit has possessed her and used her in order to demonstrate something for the sake of the Church, opening up new vistas on to the Gospels.

That, and that alone, should be the motive for the Church's interest in Thérèse. That, and that alone, should engage the attention of those who feel themselves put off by many features of her cultus, or even of her character, or who experience indefinable objections to them. In fact, there are few other cases in which it is so prudent to distinguish between the mission of a saint and its inessentials. For instance, there is one particularly noticeable and permanent characteristic of Thérèse's—her self-reflection: this cannot be counted an essential. Indeed I hope to show how unfortunate circumstances to some extent intensified this habit, and how she comes to resemble a patient in the demonstration-theatre, who follows and takes to heart the observations which the professor is making to his students about the case. She becomes inclined, therefore, to forget that she has to remain a neutral object and not to take everything personally; she takes as personal what was meant as simply objective. This means that the spectator's vision may momentarily become blurred; which proves irritating to many. It will be shown later how far Thérèse was responsible for her "self-canonization" and how far it was her own family which laid the foundations for her cult in Carmel during her very lifetime. But it is all the more important not to indulge Thérèse's inclination to self-reflection by conducting prolonged psychological analyses—rather, to stand off a little in order to keep one's gaze on the objective mission. Clearly this habit of Thérèse's makes it no easy task to do so. But, as I have insisted, it is no solution to seek for explanations solely at the personal and psychological level. Such an attempt would prove vain with every saint; but it is doubly impossible with Thérèse, whose mission it was to expound her "way". The only sure procedure is painstakingly to allow each detail of her biography to sketch out the trajectory of her mission. And this movement from the biographical and personal to the dogmatic level in the exposition of Thérèse's sanctity rests upon the authority of the Church. I have quoted Pius XI's statement on her divine mission; he goes on to describe her as "something sent down to earth from heaven as a proof of the miraculous." And he puts the question: "What is the word that God wishes to say to us? What does the little Thérèse wish to say to us, who allowed herself to be transformed into a word of God? For God speaks in her work . . ." Pius XI goes a step further in his homily at the Mass of her canonization; after having referred to the Gospels as the basis for her doctrine of spiritual childhood he continues: "The new saint, Thérèse, had thoroughly learned this teaching of the Gospels and translated it into her daily life. Moreover she taught the way of spiritual childhood by word and example to the novices of her convent. She set it forth clearly in all her writings, which have gone to the ends of the world, and which assuredly no one has read without being charmed, or without reading them again and again with great pleasure and much profit . . . In her catechism lessons she drank in the pure doctrine of faith, from the golden book of *The Imitation of Christ* she learned asceticism, in the writings of St John of the Cross she found her mystical theology. Above all, she nourished heart and soul with the inspired Word of God on which she meditated assiduously, and the Spirit of Truth taught her what he hides as a rule from the wise and prudent and reveals to the humble. Indeed, God enriched her with a quite exceptional wisdom, so that she was enabled to trace out for others a sure way of salvation." In a similar sense, the day after her canonization, Pius XI spoke of a "new message" or "new mission", and the canonization Bull itself refers to "a new model of sanctity"; in a letter the Pope speaks of her as a "master" in matters of spiritual teaching; the *decretum de tuto* for the canonization had already laid it down that the canonization "extends beyond the person of Thérèse".

Thérèse's soul is unfolded in all its breadth by the Rule and her office in the Order, but this is ultimately for the sake of the Church. The new dimension of one's being which one looks for through being born again in an Order has no other purpose for a Catholic than to make one wholly Catholic. Just as Mary's role, through the Cross, is extended to becoming Mother to all the faithful, becoming "the womb of the Church", so the Christian in an Order, through the Cross of the vows, is enabled to share in all the concerns of Christ's Church. To be at the immediate disposition of the Church is the very essence and mystery of the religious life and the ultimate justification for the vows and the Rule; the fruitfulness promised to those who abandon all is meant for the benefit of the brethren.

Those entering an Order should be aware of this function within the Church which they are undertaking; they should also be aware of the new dimension of life which they are meant to acquire through the vows. If this tension between personal sanctification and the service of the Church is lacking in an Order and the narrow personal horizons of the cloister do not open outwards onto the great objective horizons of the Church, then the whole purpose of the vows is likely to be frustrated. Thérèse not only had the good fortune to escape such frustration, she is an outstanding example of the fruitfulness which the vows can produce.

The horizons of the Church are thrown open to Thérèse's vision when she is allotted two priest-brothers. "For a long time I had harboured a desire which seemed beyond realization: to have a brother a priest. I often thought that if my little brothers had not been taken to Heaven I should have had the happiness of seeing them at the altar. I longed for this happiness! And then the good God gave me more than I had dreamed of. . . ." On the Feast of the great Saint Teresa, 1895, the little Thérèse is busy at her work—it is washing day—when the Prioress takes her aside and reads her a letter from a young seminarist, P. Adolphe Roulland, who, "inspired as he said by St Teresa, was asking for a young Sister to devote herself specially to his salvation and the salvation of the souls who would one day be entrusted to him. He promised that when he was ordained he would make a memento each day during Holy Mass for the chosen to become his sister. And I was chosen to become the sister of this future missionary." The way that Thérèse reacts to this gift is both psychologically and theologically significant: "Mother, I did not know how to express my happiness. Such an unexpected fulfilment of my desires awoke a joy in my heart which I can only describe as childlike. I have to carry my mind back to the days of my childhood to recapture such joys, so thrilling that one's soul is too small to contain them. Never had I tasted such bliss for years; I felt as though a new side of my soul had been laid bare, as if chords which had hitherto remained forgotten had now been touched." This experience opened her soul up to a strange new world. It is true that Thérèse had entered Carmel specially to pray for priests. And she knew why she was doing so; on her Italian pilgrimage she had the opportunity to observe bad priests. And two years later, when a famous Carmelite preacher apostatized, she writes to Céline: "Oh, my Céline, let us live for souls, let us be apostles, especially let us save souls of priests, souls which should be more transparent than crystal . . . Alas! how many bad priests there are . . . Céline, do you understand the cry of my heart?"

A novice says at the canonization process: "She taught us that the good God would hold a reckoning with us for the priests we ought to have saved through prayer and sacrifice but did not save because we were unfaithful and cowardly." All of this becomes completely real to her in the moment when she is ordered to stake her life for a priest who is allotted to her. Eighteen months later, in the same manner, she receives her second brother, Maurice Bellière; and this step teaches her the law inspiring every action of the Church, the law of Catholic universality. "When I pointed out that I had already offered my poor merits for one future missionary, and so did not believe I could do the same for another, you gave me this answer: that obedience would double my merits. In my heart of hearts I had thought the same; and since the zeal of a Carmelite ought to embrace the world I even hope by God's grace to be useful to more than two missionaries. I pray for all . . ." And then she places herself at the very centre of the Carmelite vocation: "Like our holy Mother, St Teresa, I wish to be a 'daughter of the Church', and to pray for all the intentions of the Vicar of Jesus Christ. That is the great aim of my life."

Thérèse had already had a vision of this universal scope of the religious life whilst she was still in the world. Unerringly she recognized the danger of becoming narrow which threatens any weak soul in the confinement of the cloister and the Rule. On her Italian pilgrimage she had deliberately allowed the beautiful scenery of God's wide world to impress itself upon her soul, storing up reserves against the narrowness of the cloister. This is the sweep of her thoughts as she gazes on a Swiss landscape from a passing train: "Then there rose up before me a picture of the religious life as it really is, with its constraints and its daily sacrifices offered up in secret. Then I understood how easy it would be to become turned in upon oneself, and to forget the sublime purpose of one's vocation. So I said to myself, 'Later on, when the time of trial comes, and I am a prisoner in Carmel, unable to see more than a little corner of the sky, I shall remember today; this scenery will give me courage. I shall no longer attach any importance to my petty concerns when I think of the power and grandeur of God; I shall love him alone and not have the misfortune to hang on to straws now that my heart foresees what is reserved for those who love him'." The world's grandeur and majesty was to remain with her in the cloister, for that is where her dreams take her: "Usually I dream of woods and flowers, of brooks and the sea. I nearly always see pretty little children, or else catch butterflies and birds such as I have never seen before." But this is all background, nothing but a symptom of her health of soul, which at a glance measures the heights to be climbed and aims directly at them. "O Mother, how beautiful our vocation is! It is up to Carmel to preserve the salt of the earth! We offer our prayers and sacrifices for the apostles of the Lord; we ourselves must be apostles, whilst they by their words and example are preaching the Gospel to our brethren. What a noble mission we have! But I must not dwell on this, I feel that my pen would run on for ever. . . . " In her vision of the Carmelite mission the little Thérèse attains the stature of the great Teresa.

An apostle of apostles, that is how Thérèse saw her vocation; and the gift of priest-brothers thrills her to the marrow; her deepest longings are awakened, the tenderest fibre of her being is stirred. Everything else in her Carmelite life, her sacrifices and self-denial, her prayers and her silence, is woven around this deep, interior secret, the heart of her Carmelite mission. Thérèse formulated few parts of her teaching so clearly as this, her mission to the Church, which is primarily concerned with the relation between contemplation and action. In a word, the mystery of *contemplation as action*. It is in virtue of this mystery that Thérèse has become the contemplative patron of Catholic Action; she stands there warning us that this Action is but "wood, hay and stubble" (1 Cor 3:12) if it is not caught up and borne along by the ground swell of contemplation. She warns us that all the busyness of the active apostle, and especially of the priest, depends for its power upon the immovable contemplative Orders. Here, in prayer and suffering, rise the springs of all Catholic Action; consequently a primary task for this Action is to found centres of contemplation. In some ways Thérèse develops her teaching about contemplative action along traditional lines, presupposing the medieval formula "*ex plenitudine contemplationis activus*" and amplifying it. But in other respects the construction she puts upon the usual formula opens up entirely new possibilities of welding contemplation and action together.

As a child Thérèse's hankering after contemplation was quite marked. When she was very small, accompanying her father on his fishing expeditions, she used to sit on the grass a little apart from him. "Then my thoughts would become most deep; and without knowing what meditation meant, my soul became deeply absorbed in true prayer. I would listen to distant sounds, the murmur of the wind. Sometimes confused notes of military music were wafted over to me from the town, and filled my heart with gentle melancholy. The earth appeared to be a place of exile, and I dreamed of heaven." Once the two of them are caught in a thunderstorm; Thérèse is thrilled with the thunder and lightning which makes "the good God seem very near". In her seventh year she sees the sea, and the sight of it overpowers her; the whole drama of it speaks to her of God. Along with her cousin Marie she plays at "hermits" in the garden: "We had nothing but a poor hut, a little patch of corn and a garden in which to grow a few vegetables. Life flowed along in unbroken contemplation; that is to say, one of us would take the other's place at prayer whenever either was called to the active life. All this was done in harmony and silence, in a manner perfectly appropriate to the religious life." About two years later she asks her older sister, Marie, who had now become her second mother in succession to Pauline, if she may be allowed to practise half an hour of mental prayer each day. Marie refuses. She then bargains for a quarter of an hour, which is likewise turned down. Marie's comment was: "She seemed to me so pious that I was anxious for her. I feared that the good God might take her to himself too quickly." But the nine-year-old child did not allow herself to be discouraged. At the Abbey School she approaches the headmistress with the request to be instructed in contemplation. The headmistress is amazed, and not a little embarrassed; clearly she found this a most difficult subject to teach. About this time, on the days when there were no lessons, Thérèse used to go into a corner of her room and pull the bed-curtains, so as to make a little cell where she could meditate. When a mistress asked her what she used to do there, she told her truthfully. "But what do you think about?" asked the good nun, laughing. "I think of the good God, of the shortness of life, of eternity; well, *I think*." Thérèse adds: "Now

I realize that I was actually practising mental prayer, my heart receiving gentle instruction from the divine Master." This adventure in contemplation reaches its climax when she makes her Communion; at this point Thérèse's finite being is assumed into God's hands: "Our meeting this day could only be described as a *fusion*! We were no longer two. Thérèse had disappeared, like the drop of water which loses itself in the immensity of the sea. Only Jesus remained. He was the Master, the King! Had Thérèse not asked him to take away her freedom?" Like all the other pupils at the Abbey School, Thérèse was taught to follow the Mass by reading the prayers in her missal. "But the dear child did not stick to it. When someone showed her which parts she was to read she used to thank them with a gracious smile, and fix her gaze upon the book for a few seconds; then she would raise her head again as if the book were a distraction."

The cloister does not alter her ways in this respect. "Apart from the Divine Office which I joyfully recite each day, despite my unworthiness, I have not the courage to set myself searching in books for beautiful prayers: there are so many, it gives me a headache! Besides, each is more beautiful than the next! Since I cannot say them all and do not know which to choose, I do the same as children who do not know how to read. I simply say whatever I wish to the good God, and he always understands me." It is as though contemplation is her centre of gravity to which she is constantly being pulled back. "Whenever the kind of work she was engaged on did not necessarily absorb her whole attention her mind turned quite naturally to God." That was in accordance with her own teaching: she insists that in the midst of activity one should still remain detached, in contemplation: "You worry yourselves too much about your tasks, as if you alone were responsible for them. Are you concerned at this moment about what is happening in other Carmels? whether the nuns there are busy or not? Does their work prevent you from praying or meditating? Well, in the same way you should banish yourself from personal tasks. Conscientiously spend the prescribed time at them, but with detachment of spirit." "I once read that the Israelites, when building the walls of Jerusalem, worked with one hand and held a sword in the other. That is what we should do; never lose ourselves completely in action. . . ." These illustrations allow us to glimpse the attraction which contemplation exercised upon the soul of Thérèse; and yet one cannot say that Thérèse was by nature predestined for a contemplative life. One witness says of her: "Sister Thérèse of the Child Jesus had an extremely active and energetic soul beneath her gentle and friendly appearance; her actions at all times bore the marks of a very strong character and a manly spirit." She feels herself strongly drawn towards action; she would gladly have become a Vincentian in order to nurse and educate orphans. Her sister Léonie declares that no amount of dirt or poverty could put her off minding children. Once, at the age of fourteen, with her heart already set on Carmel, she happens to start reading a missionary periodical. Suddenly she shuts it and explains: "I will not read it. Even as it is I have such a burning desire to go on the Missions that I must not even flick through the illustrations of this apostolate. I will enter Carmel."

Céline tells us that Thérèse followed the contemplative vocation on no other grounds than that she regarded it as the most powerful and far-reaching action. "The religious life seemed to her primarily a means of saving souls. She even thought at one time of becoming a nun in the foreign missions; but the hope of being able to save more souls by penance and sacrifice was responsible for her decision to enclose herself in Carmel. She confided the reason for her decision to me: to win more souls for Jesus by suffering. She was of the opinion that it is much harder for our natures to work without seeing the fruits of our labour, without encouragement or distraction of any kind . . . she wished to embrace this life of death, so much more profitable than others for the salvation of souls, in order, as she herself put it, to become a prisoner as soon as possible and so transmit to souls the beauty of heaven. Her very special aim in entering Carmel was to pray for priests, and sacrifice herself for the need of the Church. She called this form of the apostolate 'dealing with the chief', meaning that one reached the members through the Head." Thérèse thinks of contemplation as the ultimate source of fruitfulness, the most powerful active force in the Church and the most helpful for sinners; yet this does not mean that she allows a sort of activism to pervert the traditional view of contemplation. Thérèse's contemplation has the authetic ring to it; it involves complete surrender and an openness to the Word of the Lord reaching beyond all active prayer into total passion and suffering.

It is not the essence of her contemplation which is different but her insight into its effects; she relates them more closely to the saving work of the Church than any previous teacher had done. The Fathers, for instance, had a predominantly individualistic conception of contemplation—influenced, no doubt, by the Platonic, Aristotelian, Stoic and Neoplatonic contemplative ideals. And whilst the medieval mystics certainly do lay great stress on the fruitfulness of contemplation, they never free themselves entirely from the categories handed down to them. Spanish mysticism, on account of its psychological, self-analytical attitude, also remains largely centred upon the condition of the contemplative, however apostolic-minded it may become in practice. The little Thérèse is the first to rid contemplation of its Neoplatonic relics; this fact alone is sufficient to guarantee her place in the history of theology. In fact, though not in so many words, she has substituted the notion of fruitfulness for that of effectiveness. She is the first to see quite clearly that action is not simply an effect of overflowing contemplation (in the sense that anyone filled with wisdom can then pass over without danger into a period of action) but that contemplation in itself is a dynamic force, and is indeed the source of all fruitfulness, the first impulse in all change. This is the sense in which contemplation is more active than action, if the latter is taken to mean external deeds.

Once Thérèse is wondering what a person can do best in order to save souls; a simple sentence from the Gospels presents the key to her problem: "Lift up your eyes and see the countries, for they are white already to the harvest." And the gloss on it: "The harvest indeed is great, but the labourers are few. Pray ye, therefore, the Lord of the harvest, that he send forth labourers." Why, Thérèse asks, does our Lord humble himself so as to attend to our prayers? "Because he harbours such an incomprehensible love for us that he wishes us to share in the salvation of souls. He wishes to do nothing without us." But what form should this co-operation take? "Our vocation, yours and mine, is not to go harvesting in the fields of ripe corn; Jesus does not say to us, 'Lower your eyes, look at the fields, and go and reap them . . .' Our mission is still loftier. Here are Jesus' words, 'Lift up your eyes, and see . . .' See how in my heaven there are places empty; it is for you to fill them . . . each one of you is my Moses praying on the mountain; ask me for labourers and I shall send them, I await only a prayer, a sigh from your heart! Is not the apostolate of prayer lifted higher, so to speak, than the apostolate of preaching?

Our mission, as Carmelites, is to form those Gospel labourers, they will save millions of souls whose mothers we shall be . . . What have priests that we need envy!" Here we have a doctrine of contemplation, explicitly formulated, such as the medievals never worked out clearly, Contemplation is not superior to action because it allows a person leisure and tranquillity, as the ancients thought who depised work as illiberal. Nor even, as St Thomas argued in stating the traditional doctrine, because contemplation is directly concerned with God whereas action deals "only" with one's neighbour. It is solely because, of all the Church's manifestations of love, contemplation bears the most abundant fruit, so abundant that Thérèse does not hesitate to compare the contemplative vocation to that of the priesthood. She believes that her vocation quite literally makes her the mother of souls, an office no less dignified than that of the priest who also fulfils a family role. ("To be your spouse, O Jesus! to be a Carmelite, and, in union with you, the mother of souls.") How typical of her witty, playful mind, is the image of herself as the "little zero" which she hits upon to express her relationship to her priest-brother: "Let us work together for the salvation of souls; I of course can do very little, absolutely nothing, in fact, alone; what encourages me is the thought that by your side I can be of *some* use; after all, zero by itself has no value, but put alongside *one* it becomes potent, always provided it is put on the *proper side*, after and not before! . . . So please, Brother, be good enough to send your blessing to the *little zero* the good God has put beside you."

This fructifying contemplation is the greatest task which can be set to a Christian, and makes the highest demands. The fact that contemplation is superior to action means that it must integrate into itself the whole pathos and strength of action. What Thérèse call contemplation is the very opposite of Quietism: it is the fruit of an endeavour into which one throws all one's energies. And it has to be applied to the smallest details of everyday life if the truth of God's Word is to be brought down to earth. "Many souls say, 'I have not the strength to make this or that sacrifice'. But they should try! the good God never refuses the first grace which gives one courage to act, and if that is grasped then one can take heart and march from victory to victory." But this initial action is focused into a central act of contemplation which does not waver, but firmly directs the energies that are bent towards external action. Here Thérèse touches upon the second formula governing action and contemplation, not Thomas' formula but that of Ignatius: "*in actione contemplativus*". Except that it is better reversed in the case of the Carmelite Thérèse: "*in contemplatione activus.*" When Thérèse is entrusted with the office of novice-mistress and recognizes that it is far beyond her own powers, she does not sit down to work out a scheme for dividing her time between prayer and action. "I put myself straightaway into God's arms, and behaved like one of those children who bury their fair heads on their father's shoulder when they are frightened; I said, 'Lord, you see that I am too small to feed your little ones; if you wish me to be the means of giving each what she needs then fill my little hand; and without leaving your arms, without even turning my head, I shall distribute your precious gifts to the souls who come asking for food'." After making this prayer she finds her task much simpler: "I devoted myself more and more to uniting myself to God alone, knowing that the rest would be added unto me." Consequently Thérèse acquires an attitude which cannot be described exactly in tems of either contemplation or action; she is beyond them both in the all-embracing law of love, which governs both receptivity and fruitfulness, both Mary and Martha. This transcendent point of unity is the ultimate knowledge granted to Thérèse; her account of it concludes the second manuscript consisting of Chapters Nine and Ten, which were finished two months before her death. (The eleventh chapter, dedicated to her sister Marie, had been written previously.)

"One day, after Holy Communion, Our Lord gave me understanding of this sentence from the Canticle, 'Draw me: we will run after thee to the odour of thy ointments'. O Jesus, there is no need then to say, 'In drawing me, draw also the souls that I love'. The simple words, 'Draw me', are enough. Truly when a soul has allowed itself to be captured by the intoxicating odour of your perfumes it cannot run alone, all the souls it loves are drawn in its train;

it is a natural consequence of its attraction towards you. Just as a torrent carries after it whatever it meets on the way, bearing it into the depths of the sea, in the same way, O my Jesus, the soul which plunges into the boundless ocean of your love draws all its treasures after it! Lord, you know that these treasures are for me the souls which it has pleased you to unite to my own; you have entrusted them to me. . ." Thérèse then proceeds to comment on the longest scriptural quotation to be found in her writings, the prayer of Christ the High Priest. It is a prayer of pure contemplation since it is completely concerned with the Father's will, but also of pure action, since it expresses completely the Son's will in regard to the Father. The two wills coincide; their object is that men should be one as the Son is one with the Father, that they should be drawn to where the Son returns after accomplishing the will of the Father. Thérèse is aware of having discovered the Archimedean point beyond which passivity and activity no longer produce a dualism. "A scientist once said, 'Give me a fulcrum and a lever and I will lift the world'. What Archimedes could not obtain has been fully granted to the saints. The almighty has given them a fulcrum—*himself*! *himself alone*! And for a lever, the prayer which burns with the fire of love; that is how they have lifted the world, that is how the saints still fighting on earth lift it, and will continue to lift it till the end of time." She is beyond the dualism of passivity and activity, at the point where they meet in Christian love. "Our Lord has said, 'No man can come to me except the Father who has sent me draw him'. Then he teaches us that it is enough to knock and it will be opened, to seek, in order to find, and to stretch out one's hand humbly in order to receive." Ultimately, in fact, the two aspects, the seeking and the finding, coincide; the moment we knock is the moment we are given entry, and the more openly and passively we surrender to God's operations the more actively he works in us and we in him. "I ask Jesus to draw me into the flames of His love, to unite me so closely to himself that he lives and acts within me. I feel that the more the fire of His love inflames my heart the more I shall say, 'Draw me', and the more also will those around me *run swiftly in the sweet odour of the Beloved.*"

And now we come to the crucial point: "Yes, they will run; we shall run together; for ardent souls can never remain inactive. Certainly, like St Mary Magdalene, they sit at the feet of Jesus, listening to his sweet and burning words. Though they seem to give nothing they in fact give more than Martha, who is troubled *about many things*. Not that Jesus blames Martha for her labours, but only for being troubled; his divine Mother humbly accepted the same labours, having to prepare meals for the Holy Family. All the saints have understood this, most of all those who filled the world with the light of the Gospel teaching. Was it not in prayer that St Paul, St Augustine, St Thomas Aquinas, St John of the Cross, St Teresa and many other friends of God, acquired the wonderful knowledge which has enthralled the finest minds?" In these modest words Thérèse succeeds perfectly in restoring both contemplation and action to their true value. She justifies contemplation by basing the superiority of contemplation on its fulness, and fruitfulness, not on the fact that it empties the mind of externals. Action is also given its due because it is not made subject to contemplation. Although our Lord blames Martha, Mary the Mother of God is the standing proof that it is not for her activity; furthermore the Lazarus episode completely justifies both sisters, showing that they loved equally and are equally sanctified. Once again Thérèse is in the right as against the traditional patristic and scholastic interpretation of the Mary–Martha antithesis, which was all too strongly influenced by the prejudices of the ancient world. Aquinas, whether consciously or unconsciously, interpreted the Gospel view of action and contemplation in Aristotelian terms; the grounds he gave for the superiority of contemplation were all derived from the "philosopher", and so he gave currency to the ancient conceptions of action and contemplation (*ST* II–II. q. 192, a. 1, c.). In order to grasp the Gospel message on this subject one is well advised to ignore Aristotle and concentrate on the interpretation given to it by our Lord in his own words and deeds and in his saints.

The ideal for Thérèse did not consist in alternating from one to the other, or in balancing them, but in perfecting the two attitudes simultaneously. Whereas

Augustine loved to separate action and contemplation, Matha and Mary, Peter and John, as types of earthly and heavenly life, Thérèse cannot imagine heaven excèpt in terms of their unity. Unlike any previous saint she regards heaven as the scene for her most intense missionary activity—"It is not happiness which attracts me . . . but Love alone! To love, to be loved and to return to earth to make Love loved." "I wish to spend my heaven in doing good upon earth . . . No, I shall not be able to take any rest until the end of the world." "I feel that my mission is soon to begin, my mission of making God loved as I love him . . . to give my little way to souls." Thérèse bases this possibility on the example of the angels: "That is not impossible, because the Angels keep watch over us from the heart of the Beatific Vision." They proceed from God as his messengers, and yet never leave him. Thérèse might equally well have referred to the Son of God, who leaves his Father in heaven and yet retains the vision of his Father in the midst of his earthly activity—for his earthly activity is shaped at every moment by his vision of the Father. The ancients show no traces of this ideal which the Christian is called upon to live. One can easily understand now why the Carmelite Thérèse felt a closer kinship and union with the saint of action, Joan of Arc, than with any other saint. Their two missions are united in our Lord's saying: "At all times I do the will of the Father."

But we have still not described the precise content of Thérèse's mission, which places her beyond the action-contemplation antithesis. In order to do this we must first outline her own conception of her mission, and her place in the Church, which involves an enquiry into her doctrine of the Church. It is typical of Thérèse's existentialism that she knows no way of envisaging the Church other than from the standpoint of her own membership.

Thérèse presents her doctrine of the Church in the course of an exposition of 1 Corinthians 12–13. She penetrates deep into the meaning of this passage through her boundless longing to do everything for God that can be done. "I have become the mother of souls; that should be enough for me. Yet I feel other vocations within me; I feel within the vocation of warrior, of priest, of apostle, doctor and martyr. . . ." Then she begins to depict the unique quality of each of these missions, and then the uniqueness of the personal vocations within each type of mission. For instance, she lists the various types of martyrdom—which are clearly mutually exclusive: "I would wish to be flayed like St Bartholomew; to be plunged into boiling oil like St John; I desire like St Ignatius of Antioch to be ground by the teeth of will beasts so as to become a bread worthy of God. With St Agnes and St Cecilia I would present my neck to the executioner's sword, and like Joan of Arc at the burning stake, murmur the name of Jesus . . ." She even regrets not having been born at the time of the Anti-Christ. "My Jesus, open your book of life where the actions of your saints are recorded: each of these actions I long to have accomplished for you." In this torment, itself a magnificent preparation, she opens the Epistle to the Corinthians and immediately comes upon the doctrine about the different members of the one Body which supplement each other, and by their diversity make up the unity of the Body. "The answer was clear but it did not satisfy my longings nor give me peace." Indeed she refuses to let herself be listed in any of these diverse offices and tasks. "In meditating on the mystical body of the holy Church I could not recognize myself in any of the members described by St Paul, or rather I wished to recognize myself in them all." So hesitatingly, but hopefully, she moves on from the twelfth to the thirteenth chapter, which opens up the supreme way of love. "The Apostle explains that even the most perfect gifts are nothing without *Love*, that charity is the most excellent way of arriving at God . . . At last I had found rest . . . *my vocation is love*!" Love is the central organ of the mystical body, the heart. Therefore it is much more than a single organ, it is the source of life for all the others: "Love alone is capable of setting the other members in motion and if love were ever to die out, then the Apostles would cease to proclaim the Gospel and the martyrs refuse to shed their blood." Just as a watch will stop if the spring is broken, so the whole action of the Church would come to a standstill if the contemplative love at the heart of it all were to cease. And so love increases in the life of each and every vocation, because it is essentially universal: "I realized that love includes every vocation, that love is all, that it embraces all times and all places, because it is eternal." And Thérèse situates herself in this universal centre: "Then, beside myself with joy, I cried out, 'O Jesus, my love! at last I have found my vocation! *my final vocation is love*. I have found my place in the bosom of the Church and it is you, my God, who have given me this place—in the heart of my Mother, the Church, *I will be love*! Thus I shall be all things; thus shall my dream be realized."

We have already learnt how this love was to become universal; in this "life of death"; in wiping out subjectivity by the vows, the Rule, and authority; in hollowing out her own personality until she became simply a "bowl" from which others might be fed, simply the kernel for others' fruit, the "zero" rounding off all unity. It is precisely through being zero, through accepting her complete unimportance, that the miraculous, total fulfilment of grace is accomplished. "I am nothing but a weak and helpless child; but it is my very weakness which gives me the courage to offer myself as a victim of your love, O Jesus . . . and love has chosen me as a holocaust, poor and imperfect creature that I am! Is this choice not worthy of love? Certainly, for in order to be completely satisfied love must stoop even to nothingness and transform this nothingness in the fire." Through the all and nothing of her own mission Thérèse has to discover the communion of saints in love.

The communion of saints is the community of grace, and therefore of love; because all love is fruitful each member is indebted to the love of the others: "In heaven we shall never be greeted with stares of indifference; for all the elect will recognize how they owe each other the graces which have brought them glory."

There each will be proud of the others, whereas no one will claim any merit for himself. "But how clearly we shall see that everything comes from the good God. The glory that I shall possess will be an unmerited grace, which does not even belong to me—and everyone will see themselves in the same light." But since love is the root of all merit, as well as its fruit, and never seeks its own, Thérèse lives more for others and in others than for herself. She who had been promised universal love now expounds one of her most remarkable ideas.

" 'Use the riches that make men unjust, to find yourselves friends who may receive you into everlasting dwellings.' As a child of light I understood that my desires to be everything and embrace every vocation were riches which might well make me unjust; so I used them to make friends. Remembering the prayer of Elisha to the prophet Elijah when he asked him for his double spirit, I presented myself before the angels and the company of the saints, and I said, 'I am the least of creatures, I know my own worthlessness, but I also know how much noble and generous hearts love to do good; therefore I beseech you, blessed inhabitants of the heavenly city, to adopt me as your child; all the glory you help me to acquire will be yours; deign to hear my prayer. I entreat you to obtain for me your *double portion of love*!' "

So Thérèse wishes to add the love of the other saints to her own love. Beside her own spirit she wishes to possess the spirit of the martyr, of the doctor of the Church, and so on; nor will this double spirit be a divided one—it will be entirely her own, as the spirit of Elisha was his own, and just as the spirit of John the Baptist was his own yet still the spirit of Elijah. However, this concentration of the spirit of all the saints in Thérèse is simply the necessary counterpart to the outpouring of her own spirit upon the spirits of the saints. "I realized that love includes every vocation, that it is all in all . . . thus I shall be all, *thus* will my dream be fulfilled." The result is complete communism in all goods and graces, which at the same time preserves the uniqueness of persons and their special missions. It is Thérèse's special mission to insist upon this communism, which is like the circulation of blood, making them all blood relations. "All those above are my blood relations! With the virgins we also shall be virgins, and doctors with the doctors, martyrs with the martyrs, because all the saints are our relations." Henceforth communism of merits is the rule: "When we are suffering through knowing that we are incapable of doing good, our only remedy is to offer the good works of others. That is the benefit of the communion of saints." This form of community became a very real personal experience for Thérèse when she resolved to renounce possession even of her private thoughts and insights. "Our own deepest personal thoughts, the fruits of our intellect and heart, constitute a treasure to which we quickly become attached, and which no one is supposed to touch . . . But I have received the grace of being no more attached to the goods of heart and spirit than to earthly goods. If I happen to say or think anything which pleases my Sisters, I find it perfectly natural for them to take it over as if it belonged to them; this thought belongs to the Holy Spirit, not to me." Thérèse develops this thought, after saying: "God has granted me this grace of penetrating into the deep secrets of love . . ." At this depth not only do the divisions between one person and another vanish, but the laws of nature no longer apply—difficult and easy, great and little, important and unimportant lose their usual meaning. "Sister Mary of the Eucharist wished to light the candles for a procession. She had no matches with her, and when her gaze fell upon the little lamp burning in front of the relics she went towards it. At first there was nothing but a weak glimmer at the end of the charred wick. Nevertheless she managed to get her candle burning and use it to light all the community's candles. Then I said to myself, 'Who could glory in their own works? See how a little, flickering lamp has produced these beautiful lights, which in their turn could light innumerable others, indeed could set the whole world ablaze. And yet that little lamp remains the cause of this burst of fire.' It is exactly the same in the community of saints. A quite tiny spark could set off great lights in the Church, doctors and martyrs for instance. And often the graces and illuminations we receive are to be attributed to some hidden soul. For the good God wishes the saints to communicate grace to each other, by their prayers, so that they shall love each other in Heaven with great love, love much greater than love within a family, even the most ideal family on earth." It will be "love of gratefulness", but also the love which finds in the beloved the fruit of its own love. "Who knows whether the joy we shall experience at the sight of the glory of the great saints, through being aware that we have contributed to it under God's providence, who knows whether this joy will not be as intense as—perhaps even sweeter than—the bliss which they themselves enjoy?" Once more Thérèse is confronting us with that "double spirit" which transcends the limits of persons.

We have finally come to the point where all our preconceptions as to great and small fail us. The differences between great and small are not overcome, however, in the kingdom of God by levelling out but by fulfilment. To level out personal differences and gifts would be an empty caricature of the true community of the saints. In her childhood Thérèse had already been worried as to "why the good God does not give all his saints the same glory". At that time Pauline had filled two vessels with water, one large and one small, and explained that in heaven everyone is filled to the brim "so that the least of the elect cannot envy the happiness of the greatest". Yet this answer, which forestalls all subsequent questions, remains fundamentally individualistic; for the time being it might set the child at rest, but in the long run it could not satisfy her thirst for souls. The next step was to transfer the locus of sanctity away from the subject into the will of God: "In the lives of the saints we see how many of them have left nothing behind them after their deaths—not the least souvenir, nor a single written line. But others again, such as our holy Mother Teresa, have enriched the Church with their sublime teaching . . . which is most pleasing to our Lord? It seems to me that either is equally pleasing to him." Even more incisively: "I understood that our Lord's love reveals itself just as well in a simple soul, which in no way resists his grace, as in the sublimest soul. Indeed, since it is the essence of love to abase itself, if all souls were to resemble those Holy Doctors who have enlightened the Church, it would give the impression that God did not stoop low enough in coming to them. But he has also created the little child who knows nothing and can only utter feeble cries; he has created the poor savage whose only guide is the natural law; and it is even to their hearts that he deigns to stoop." Once more the fact that standards of great and small no longer apply exactly in heaven has nothing to do with "making everyone equal", not even "levelling upwards". It is God's marvellous doing, as Paul showed long ago: "God hath tempered the body together, giving to that which wanted the more abundant honour, that there might be no schism in the body: but the members might be mutually one for another" (1 Cor 12:24–5). Thérèse has given us a charming picture of this mutual care between great and small: "And do you not think that when the great saints see what they owe to little souls they will love them with an incomparable love? There, I am sure, will be delightful and surprising friendships. The favourite of an Apostle or a great doctor may be a little shepherd boy; and the intimate friend of a patriarch, a simple little child. Oh how I long to be in that kingdom of love!" And the whole of this mutual care, in Thérèse's teaching, is based upon "gratitude", loving and serving one another, and being fruitful. Without fruitfulness, which means co-operating in the work of redemption, there is no community of saints.

Consequently Thérèse immediately puts these truths into practice; she offers vicarious penance for her brothers, for Christians, indeed for all men. As always, she brings it straight down to earth, into concrete detail. When she is already seriously ill she goes for a daily walk in the garden, despite the intense strain, because the Infirmarian had recommended it. Another Sister remarks that she would be better resting in her cell. "That is very true," she replies, "but do you know what gives me the strength? I offer each step for a missionary; I am thinking that there may be one over there, far away, tired out by his apostolic labours; and to lessen his fatigue, I offer mine to God." The doctor ordered her tonics: "I am convinced that these expensive medicines are useless for curing me. But I have made an arrangement with the good God by which he will bestow their benefits upon the poor missionaries who have neither the time not the means to look after themselves." And again: "I feel that the good God wishes me to suffer. The remedies, which ought to do me good, and do alleviate other patients' sufferings, only make me worse." One hot July day, just before her death: "Just now the Sisters in the laundry must be very tired. I besought the good God to strengthen them, so that the work might go peacefully and serenely. And since I was feeling so ill I was glad to be able to suffer like them." And even during her hidden wrestling with the dark powers of death: "Something is taking place within me; I am suffering, not for myself, but for another soul . . . and the Devil is angry."

Throughout all this, until the very last, it is the mystery of the "double spirit". Her soul is disposed so that not only does our Lord suffer and love with her and in her, but she also suffers and loves with her brothers, in their place. In her suffering she relieves their suffering, in her loving she bestows love upon them. Truly the spirit of contemplation makes her present everywhere—"So I shall become everything." And the same spirit which leads her to sink down into sheer powerlessness so that God may arise in all his power, that spirit gives her a share in his power over all things. "Lord, I cannot carry my demands further, I should fear to be crushed beneath the weight of my audacious desires! My excuse is found in my title of *child*; children do not analyse the meaning of their words." And yet this child knows precisely what it wants. It not only wishes to overstep the bounds of nature, but even the bounds of grace which fix the diversity of gifts within the Church. The other saints, who are each granted particular charisma, together constitute the Body of the Church. Not so Thérèse. Thérèse is not to be localized. She will be everywhere and nowhere. She wishes to make herself felt throughout the whole house, like the aroma of Christ; she will be—and this is perhaps her shrewdest description of herself—a light, a ray issuing from the brow of her Mother, the Church:

> Now, then, I am a child of Holy Church. The Church is Queen since she is your Bride, oh divine King of Kings! It is not riches and glory—not even the glory of heaven—that my heart longs for. Glory belongs by right to my brothers, the angels and the saints. My glory for me will be the reflection shining from the brow of my Mother.

# 3. The Perfectibility of Man

"What is man? About himself he has expressed, and expresses, many divergent and even contradictory opinions. In these he often exalts himself as the absolute measure of all things or debases himself to the point of despair. The result is doubt and anxiety. The Church understands these problems . . . Sacred Scripture teaches that man was created 'in the image of God', is capable of knowing and loving his creator, and was appointed by him as master of all earthly creatures."—*Pastoral Constitution on the Church in the Modern World*, I, 1, 12.

## *Contradictory Man and Religion*

### The Imperfectibility of the Creature

Man sees himself as the sum and perfect image of the cosmos. All the realms and genera of living things converge in him; no animal species is alien to him. He contains them all, as superseded and discarded forms in which he can mirror himself and, as in fables, recognize the features of his own character. Even scholastic embryology made the discovery that in his ontogenesis man recapitulates the stages of the natural development from which he emerged, which is confirmed by modern paleontology and biology. In this respect the man of today is no more and no less closely bound up with the natural cosmos and the universe than the man of mythical ages and of antiquity, who also thought of himself as a *microcosm.*

If this is so, however, it is obviously not as the result of an external summation of separate cosmic realities: he is, as their epitome, neither plant nor animal nor anything else apart from himself. "Micro" also suggests a kind of concentration, which both makes man the synthesis of the world and raises him above it. In this exaltation above the immediate he is that which mediates itself to itself; he is mind and person. He looks openly into the openness of being in general, which, of its nature, is bounded only by nothingness. Although he is always a single individual, his nature is orientated toward being in general. He receives his freedom from it and in relation to it: freedom from any constraining bond of special being appropriate to his individuality. These appropriate elements do exist, of course, but only so that they may be illuminated and liberated in the whole.

This openness of his situation and the directing of his gaze inward does not detach man's mind from the ground of nature, but enables him to make his roots in it stronger, profounder, more intimate. Animals are swept away by the waves of sexual drive which ebb and flow like the sea, whereas man can experience *eros* in a more inward, sublimated way and, through love, make for it a lasting abode in his enlightened heart. He can also do the opposite (as the German romantics well knew), and transfer the infinities of spiritual dimensions to the dark maternal forces of nature, thus giving back to them, through his spirit, the dignity that nature had accorded him. For nature was never without spirit in man, just as the human child never ascends up from lower nature to become a spiritual being, but always awakes out of profound mental depths to consciousness and freedom.

How can such a being be perfectible? Man, as the

epitome of the world, would be perfectible only if the world fulfilled itself with him and in him. But inasmuch as he transcends the world as spirit and is open to being in general, the fulfilment of the world is not enough to bring about his perfection. Man is personal, transcending the world and its being. The personal is more than being, which is predicable of a multiplicity of things; it is unique. It is that which existentially justifies the unrepeatable finality of exclusive love. Although every man is a person, and thus possesses this quality of incomparability, it cannot be predicted of him as a quality of his being. As spiritual beings men have in common many qualities which are of the species; but in those same spiritual beings, inasmuch as they are persons, these qualities are so different that subsumption under one generic term is impossible.

If the question of perfectibility is asked—at this stage, purely formally—then one thing is certain: the person does not disappear into the race, however, the total final purpose is interpreted—statically or dynamically, or in terms of a materialistic, biologistic, or even theologico-mystical evolution. Such a subordination of the person to the world's being is as equally inadmissible as the contrary "acosmistic" (Scheler's word) conception of the person, which sees its perfectibility as something which is possible only beyond the world's being (and hence, logically, beyond its own corporality).

The nature of human love shows how indissolubly intellectual being and the personal are bound up with each other. Both in his natural being and his personal being man finds his completion and his happiness only in communion with another human being. This is the basis of the sexual difference (in which the profoundest wisdom is revealed), devised by *natura naturans* for the most intimate encounter and unity. It lies at the heart of the nature of the species, and roots it in *eros;* through the natural difference itself it shows man the eternally unbridgeable, unimaginable difference between one spiritual being and another. And again, this—rightly—exclusive love does not exhaust a person's relations with the world.

Man (as a cognitive, conative being), in spite of any individual tie to another person, remains open to the whole world, that is, to a world of work, a world of research, a world to be built up and realized in the human community. In addition, in order to remain open to the world, he remains open to the whole realm of being beyond it, which he misunderstands if he tries to embrace it as the quantitative sum of "world material" and thus undertakes interplanetary expansions of his area of habitation and power. He makes this "technical" plunge into the quantitative only because a philosophical plunge into the qualitative is doomed from the start. The search for the eternal "realm of spirits", the epitome of the qualitative personal, was a dream that Leibniz, Herder, the young Schiller, Hölderlin, Novalis, and Hegel dreamed, but, obviously, did not carry into their waking thoughts.

Neither the other person as the beloved, chosen one, nor the universe as a place of work and achievement, nor the unattainable totality of all persons answers man's deepest needs. Ultimately, it is only Absolute Being, itself spiritual and personal, that can do that, beyond the difference between spirit and nature, beyond the even profounder difference between the personal (as absolute uniqueness) and being (as absolute universality and totality). Within man no transition is possible between the two poles.

Don Juan tried to bridge the gap by starting from the person and thus destroyed his very starting point: the fidelity and exclusivity of the love between one person and another. The pantheist tries to do it by starting from the universe to which he transfers personal love; this can lead only to an illusory intoxication. The average man resigns himself early to a compronise between the two halves of life which can never be completely integrated: friendship and study, family and the office, private and political life. In renouncing the possibility of ever making his life whole, man can draw a certain satisfaction from the fact that these two spheres, although never fully penetrating each other, can complement and enrich each other. This unresolved tension can engender a sense of life which saves him from narrowness and rigidity and always offers him the possibility of a new departure.

This unbridgeable gap in man's nature affects also his relationship to God. Wholeness would be possible if the inwardness of the natural and spiritual love-relationship and the sovereign freedom of the abstract knowledge and shaping of the world could be united within an inclusive third relation which would be not only the origin, but also the final goal, of the other two. Quasi-infinite love is possible between two finite beings only if infinite love is operative in the ground of their nature, that is, if that which the lovers swear to each other is not necessarily an intoxicated exaggeration, or a "trick of nature" (for which she subsequently offers a cynical explanation), or else *hubris* (which causes a tragic fall). Equally, if a spiritual being loses himself in the abstract demands of a political or technical world of work, it is no betrayal of his mind to a mere anonymous, antlike existence, made palatable by promises of a utopian future, not for man as a person, but as a species. The individual will maintain mental honesty if, behind and above the objective spirit to which he has to sacrifice himself, there is an infinite mind toward which, in all the activities of his freedom, of his control and service of the world, he is moving, with the same or even greater intensity of love than that which he has experienced in the bosom of parents, family, marriage, and friendship.

The happiness caused by such a momentary vision of the possible wholeness of life within a religious relationship, the unimaginable promise it seems to contain, fades into inadequacy as soon as we try to reach for it directly. It is not enough to indicate the place where the higher third entity must find itself if existence is to be completed; for the question remains whether, as it is constituted, it *can* be completed. If, however, it cannot be completed in its totality, according to its whole basic structure, then all partial, fragmentary fulfilments avail it nothing. Any partial significance is constantly combatted and, rightly, negated by the lack of meaning of the whole. The man, who doubts and despairs, who constantly exposes any partial significance of love or knowledge or virtue or achievement as meaningless because of the overall meaninglessness, cannot be refuted. If, however, man is merely a fragment and as such incapable of completion, then it would be better if he did not exist at all, and he has no other choice than to curtail and reduce his own contradictory being to the point at which the contradictions fall away and he can achieve, on a lower, more modest level, some kind of completability.

Nor is this disquieting problem solved if man imagines the idea of an infinite god as the horizon toward which his finiteness can integrate itself. It only seems to become all the more disquieting. How could God, infinite, hence in need of nothing and blissful in himself, help the integration of this creature which, from the whole structure of its being, is obviously incapable of being integrated? For its being is not only finite and in the world; it is mortal. Death, it would appear, is the great rock thrown across the path of all thinking which might lead to completeness. Even if one regards its terrible aspect as something which was a subsequent development in original nature, the ending of man's earthly life poses one insistent question: How can a natural being, which must necessarily die (as he must as part of a genus and a race), be conceived as united, to the point of identity, with an infinite spiritual and personal being with infinite claims of knowledge and love?

The question is not answered by saying that man is made up of a "mortal" body and an "immortal" soul; the division is a different one: that between the cosmic mind-soul of nature and the "supercosmic" person in direct relation to God. It is also a falsification to see the cosmic soul, with Origen, as a state of self-alienation of the spirit. The acts in which the mind-soul experiences, knows, and loves in the world have at least their uncorrupted, purely creaturely side, by virtue of which they contain eternity and are unrepeatable. However indissolubly (according to Augustine) vanity and futility may have become involved in the form of creation, thus making earthly life forever a mystery, the pure original shape of creation, now unreconstructable, was itself a hieroglyph.

The centaurlike being, man, manifests something uncompletable which points beyond himself to a manner of integration—undiscoverable to him by himself alone—which is formally indicated in the relation to God. But the manner of integration is left open and, indeed, must be left open, if the relationship between God and man is to be determined and shaped in dramatic dialogue by God alone.

## The Contradiction of Death

In death the uncompletability of man becomes obvious to the point of absurdity, because his descent into corruption destroys any vague remaining hope of integration. When the beloved face loses its colour and starts to decay, a curtain is lowered which separates forever: a unique being has gone, irrevocably. No transmigration of souls, no reunion on "other planets", is a satisfactory substitute for continuation. But death, attacking the sense of life at its core, is not simply an external catastrophe, the Fates cutting the thread. It seems to reveal a whole gradient in life that falls away in the opposite direction from wholeness.

Death is neither an external accident, nor is it comprehensible—in its opposition to the sense of life—as a constituent element of being, however desperately one may try to show this. After all, one cannot swear eternal faithfulness with a time limit set to it. The only reason that hearts do not constantly rebel against the dark omnipotence of death is that its fateful wind has always bent the trees of the soul toward it, that the powers of infidelity, of injustice, of betrayal, of spiritual debility and physical illness and infirmity are familiar to us from childhood in all their destructive strength. They are forces that are not only above us, but in us, with whom we seem inexplicably to have made a compact, voluntarily, yet against our will, at a time and place we can no longer remember.

This is Kafka's problem: How do these alien forces, the worst of which is guilt, first come to us from without, then penetrate us layer by layer, until we are "compelled" to acknowledge them as our own corruption and declare, "I am guilty"? The horror of their alienness nevertheless remains. Therefore, the heart that has to confess itself as sinful—not adventitiously, but by reason of its very nature—is always close to rebellion against the existence that has been forced on it. It casts around for a tribunal to release it from this sentence of doom which can only have been spoken by a "God".

But in the meanwhile these powers claim the whole man; let him turn which way he will, he cannot escape them. He has been unable to awake to the consciousness of his dignity and his mission without already finding the worm in him that gnaws at the kernel of his freedom and love. He recognizes a moral imperative, not just as an indifferent law to which he is subject, but as that which will lead him to his true freedom. But he also feels an unwillingness to follow this lead, a laziness that weighs him down, a sluggishness of the heart that would rather abide by itself than embark on the strenuousness of love. Love means self-conquest, and so even as a child one seeks a way of having the pleasure of love without self-conquest. He wants to win the affection of the world without exerting the self; this is the essence of non-love disguised as love; this is lust.

This fateful sense of not being able to do something and not wanting to do it, from which the child who starts to experience sin for the first time tries violently to escape, is a prelude to the inexorable objective forces, whose deceitfulness the heart detects at once. Learning that radical protest is useless, the heart is finally overpowered by their crushing weight. The world of the adults is right, and wrongness is obviously an integral part of this world. And I myself am moving towards this world of adulthood, and therefore must come to terms with injustice. There may be attempts in this world, both in the private and in the public sphere, to dam in the destructive powers; to associate oneself with these attempts will be noble and praiseworthy, but nowhere, either privately or publicly, will man be able to deal finally with the hydra. He carries it around with him as his enemy; it grows with him, and often it seems to him as if, with the growing effort to conquer it and transform the world into a paradise, the snake head doubles itself after every blow.

In the region where he imagines he can register something like real "progress", in the organization of a moral world order, this so-called progress seems only to open up apocalyptic abysses. Measurable progress, not only in the technological, but also in the cultural and social fields, can, of its nature, take place only within the natural order of humanity. But the depth of a person's individuality, whose home is in the eternal, resists being reduced to a means within a type. The progress of optimism of a technological culture has to make so much noise because it has to drown ever more desperate cries of the ravished person. Even such an anti-socialist as Nietzsche, who appears to have been concerned only with single outstanding individuals, in the critical moment, reassessed all personal values through nature and reduced them to biology. The superman has to be "bred", and for this purpose are all moral valuations (which disclose in us a profound incapacity for good, what Kant called the radically bad) to be dissolved into a real biological strength. That Nietzsche's ideas lead inevitably to those of his bitterest opponents, history has shown and, thereby, indicated also that the problems Neitzsche was rightly concerned about can be solved only on a basis other than his.

## The Answer of Religion to the Conflict

Man would not be man if he were not constantly aware of the essential conflict, which the increasingly grave state of the world only renders more acute. Sucked ever more sinisterly into optimistic, hopeful schemes for world improvement, for unravelling the mystery of man, and dominated ever more fully by the collusive and apparently inescapable forces of economics, world politics, and world technology, he sees with horror the danger to his last remaining shreds of freedom and of personal feeling. These powers in a dreadful conspiracy offer him, instead of true joy, true suffering, true fidelity, and true self-sacrifice, only bogus versions the validity of which rests on a tacit betrayal of the eternal person.

The critical world situation, however, is just a

frightening illumination of what it means to be human. If it emerged from the foregoing that man can become finally whole and integrated, that his nature can be given a formal expression, but never a specific content—because the requisite synthesis of the elements cannot be achieved in an observable way—then this is infinitely more true of man in his fallen condition. The idea of wholeness which he can conceive of himself not only surpasses his nature; it contradicts it. However he may put this idea into practice, there will always be one forgotten element that has to be included, because the conflict is rooted indissolubly in the very nature of the man seeking wholeness.

I shall offer a short survey of the possible ways to wholeness which, insofar as they are conceived by man, can be reduced to two main ones. The third way, which overcomes the conflict, can only be conceived and offered by God and as such is correctly called "revelation", however much the other ways may claim this designation for themselves. Many men, indeed whole peoples and cultures, can believe them to be "revelation", inasmuch as they truly demonstrate an aspect of the process of becoming whole, with a clarity unattainable by the common run of men. They do not, on that account, need to be true "revelations", because, being rational, they are adequately explained by the rational faculty of man. In fact, they cannot ultimately be "revelation" because they do not unravel the Gordian knot of life; they cut through it.

This is not to say that, at the level of a preliminary conception of redemptive revelation, they do not, purely formally, adumbrate the revelation which is to proceed from God. It is a defining of the area in which the event must take place if man is truly to be the recipient of such saving revelation. The human imagination will seek to fill this formal framework with concrete preparatory conceptions, with myths of saving deities, which make clear what is to happen, and to transfer them from the region of mere thought and phantasy to the sphere of reality. It is not, however, accidental that such myths fail to emerge on the stage of actual human history. Thus, they retain an aesthetic element which is part of their magic, but also, because they are magic, they retain part of their incapacity to provide salvation. The fact that such myths exist shows the impossibility of man's achieving wholeness for himself purely anthropologically. Nor does it help to disregard myth (as a self-alienation of the spirit) in order to seek the solution in finite existence. There is no way back behind myth, but only forward beyond it, so as to arrive at the reality, which at the same time provides the integration, the possibility of which myth had hoped for.

## *Human Ways Out and the Christian Way*

### The Way of Appearance

If the paths that humanity has taken toward salvation, i.e. toward a relationship with God, are examined, the first thing to be noted is that both in their inventive conception (theory) and in their existential living out (practice) they represent the boldest conceptions and most exalted endeavours of the human spirit, borne through history by individuals and peoples prepared to sacrifice their lives for them. On no account are they to be condemned *a priori* as deceptions of the devil or is the mind that conceived them to be branded as a *fabrica idolorum*, even if these paths prove, in the event, to be fragmentary and unable to provide total, objectively indivisible salvation. They are, therefore, in a sense ambiguous. As serious attempts to discover salvation, they may contain redeeming grace hidden within them, yet as human creations they may involve man still deeper in his corruptions. What we see here is not how God directs the heart of the individual, but how the objective attempt is related to the objective problem of humanity.

The first way consists in a soaring movement of the heart, which leaves the whole of contradictory earthly existence beneath it in order to seek a home in the region of a supraterrestrial divine power. The basic idea is a very simple one: all multiplicity is opposed to unity and has in some mysterious way fallen away from it: only unity can be true being. Thus the difference between God and the world, between unity and multiplicity, is the same as that between true and untrue being, between being and appearance. Time and space confirm at every moment the inability of things to exist in place side by side and the readiness with which they change into one another. They are Sansara, driven by the power of Maya and Tršna, the unquenchable thirst for the other. The way of salvation demands an inner renunciation of worldly differences: theoretically, in the act of seeing through them all to their identical divine ground; practically, in the act of renouncing satisfaction through a finite, particular being.

What in this system can still be called love is fidelity to the *thou*, not in its difference, but in its ultimate identity with the loving self. The person loves, not out of the differentiating point of selfhood, but out of the world-transcending identity of God, only experiencing deep "compassion" for the still imprisoned individuality. But compassion, too, is robbed of its real content, because there can only be true compassion so long as the conpassionate being exists together with the object of compassion in the world in a condition of differentiation. Leaning back from regained identity into the sphere of differentiation can only have symbolic value. The ways of salvation that operate with the idea of appearance, that is, with the unreality of the fatal conflict and hence of death itself, certainly bear witness to an exalted intrepidity of the spirit, which challenges the totality of the world and its laws in order to negate them with sovereign freedom. But this negation is directed against the very nature of man, who saves his truth (in the absolute) only by abandoning his whole worldly reality.

India has been the most radical exponent of this

way and has declared all individuality, all separateness, mere appearance. But even the salvation ideas of the Greeks also, even if they stop short of the ultimate Asiatic conclusion, tend in this direction the monism of Parmenides as well as the dualism of Plato (which abandons corporeal existence in order to save only man's "immortal soul"); the central cosmic fire of the Stoics, of which the individual is only a spark which has leaped out (*scintilla animae*) and is striving to get back to its centre; above all, the Neoplatonic ideas of the lessening of being by emanation, whereby the salvation of man can be conceived only as either a dissolution of the degrees (*Nous-Psyche-Hyle*) in the supraspiritual one (*Hen*) or as the giving back at death of all the separate elements of man to the appropriate sphere.

All these forms of salvation, however different they may appear to be, have one thing in common: they endeavour to rescue something "immortal" in man by abandoning the rest to the devouring powers. That which is rescued is called the "real", that which is abandoned is called the "unreal". However beautiful and sublime this may seem in theory, practice throws a rather different light on it, because it is no longer worthwhile committing oneself finally and responsibly to the transient. Moreover, insofar as these systems place the "immortal" element on the side of the divine, they are basically Asiatic: a reciprocity of love between God and man is not a serious possibility. It is only possible for as long as man in the conflict of existence is different from God, for as long as he can experience God as grace from the divine sphere, a hand reached out to him, and (with the Stoics) rids himself of those resistances which prevent him from attuning himself to the great law of the universe.

If the renunciation of finite pleasure is attractive in its heroism, we must remember that its purpose is to overcome the conflict and thus get rid of pain. But perhaps the renunciation of pain, from the point of view of the possible wholeness of man, is more dangerous than the renunciation of pleasure. The Greeks felt this and therefore preferred, at least in the classical age, to accept ultimate contradictions between a logically thought-out metaphysical antropology and the particular conditions of earthly life. They did not, in the cause of achieving human wholeness, want to draw out conclusions which ultimately cancel out man. Their thinking remains so close to reality that the metaphysical perspectives do not ultimately throw doubt on this reality, but rather impart to it something like a transfiguring halo. Thus, the relation between transient and eternal existence remains curiously unresolved.

Only on this basis was tragedy possible. Man is committed, to the point of sacrificing himself, to the order of the gods, but the order of the gods remains committed to man and is often, on his account, drawn with him into conflict. If the world is "appearance", then it is appearance which is beloved of the gods themselves. The tragedy of conflict is not overcome, as in India, by denying it, but is the necessary prerequisite for the purification of the heart (*catharsis*). Thus, all remains in a dreamlike fashion with the understanding that the question of ultimate reality cannot be raised.

## The Way of the Tragic Conflict

This brings us to the second possible way. The contradictory nature of existence is so fundamental that the problem of salvation must be concerned with it. It cannot be left out of account in trying to solve the question of salvation. The way which called it appearance cancelled out the good as well as the bad. What makes life profound and noble, if not suffering and tragedy? What steels man and polishes the hidden jewel, if not suffering? And not just some external, contingent and avoidable suffering, but the essential suffering involved in being man. In mutual exaltation of nature and spirit—in spite of all the mutual threat—lies that incomparable sublimity that neither animals nor "God" can achieve. This incomparable quality of being set about with abysses is what makes us shudder in Shakespearean tragedy at the sight of the monstrous thing that is man. Or in Faust, who both says and does not say to the passing moment, "Tarry a while, thou art so fair", and ultimately, in his eternal striving, is already redeemed.

Even more than Greek tragedy the world of the Germanic heroes shows man's tragic situation as that which most perfectly characterizes him. It is not the modern idea of man's being divided against himself, but a sense of grandeur, which is imparted, not only by the tragic downfall, but by the indissolubility of fidelity and loyalty. However meaningless it may appear in view of the downfall, through the downfall it gains its eternal lustre, which makes it continue as an inspiration, to be celebrated in song, in the memory of following generations. The mythical realm of the gods which arches over such a picture of the earth can itself be only a reflection of the most sublime earthly qualities. Even the realm of the eternal ones is riven by mortal struggles and is full of battles and cataclysmic downfalls which cannot be smoothed away by ideas of astronomical cosmic cycles and philosophical theories of an eternal return.

But the distinguishing human quality would not emerge from this view of the world if in the values of loyalty (and of its opposite, treachery) the ethical did not everywhere prevail and was not stronger than sheer vital energy. Here, too, man stands within the framework of that which is the right of the order of the clan; thus, it is the figure between right and wrong that is transposed into the absolute.

Hence, one cannot condemn dualistic systems, however meaningless they may ultimately appear to be. Marcionism, for example, which makes the biblical opposition of law and grace (as of the Old and the New Testament) an absolute one between two divinities, reflects within the conceptual framework of Gnosticism an ubiquitous anthropology. It can receive different emphases. For it may be that man, by nature the creation of the dark god of the world, rebels against his mortally contradictory laws and precisely thus—with the grace of the supreme god—is able to break through into the realm of freedom and the spirit. Marcionism, then, is only a dramatic form of the way of salvation, already discussed, from multiplicity to unity.

It may be, however, that man becomes the victim of the struggle of the two divinities, and only in death is able to wrest himself away from the god of the world and fly to the arms of the paternal god of grace and freedom. This is that fascinating mixture of Gnosticism and Christianity which crops up in many Protestant variants—at its purest, perhaps, in the poems of Blake, but also quite clearly in the dramas of Schiller, where the tragedy of breaking through a realm of right, now superseded and thus put in the wrong, into a realm of freedom reveals the shape and meaning of existence. However much the tragic hero by his breakthrough makes life in this realm of freedom possible for the generations that come after, this secured freedom still remains insignificant and wearisome. All human greatness is concentrated in the struggle of the breakthrough, in which death and birth form an indissoluble unity.

It is never far to Parsee and Manichean-Catharist dualism when the situation of a struggle and break-through is taken as the primary condition of man. Such systems of metaphysics can only be meant as foils for an aristocratic, heroic view of man. If one makes absolute the struggle which is at the very heart of existence (important also in great pre-Socratic philosophies such as those of Heraclitus and Empedocles), and is to be conceived and carried out as a supreme idea, he requires a man who, tried by suffering and resistance, has learned to love the furnace of pain which is purifying him and despises any cheaper harmonizing process.

Nietzsche, who opposes any eschatological elimination of suffering with his "eternal return" which eternally reintegrates it, sees in this an antipessimistic ideal which affirms everything that strengthens one: "In pain there is as much wisdom as in pleasure; they are both among the chief forces which preserve the race"; "pain is a necessary ingredient of all activity; there is a will to suffer at the basis of all organic life." Unlike the way of appearance, which in the first place seeks to eradicate suffering and thus sets about destroying "thirst" (concupiscence), the way of the tragic struggle never loses touch with historical reality. It offers no suspension in empty space, but ensures that the foot that kicks against the stone knows it is kicking against that which is truly real, of which it partakes.

## The Provisional Nature of Both Ways

No one, however, was foolish enough to proclaim the way of suffering as the way to God, as if the more pain one endured, the closer he came to the absolute. Pain remains, at best, an episode; only in its purifying and tempering power in the comprehensive whole of life in this world, which is taken as the uncrossable horizon, as the "divine", is it to keep its assured place. "Divinity is day and night, winter and summer, war and peace, being satisfied and being hungry; it changes like oil mixed with perfumes" (Heraclitus). Therefore, this way of the "immortal struggle" (Plato) is basically not a way, but a self-knowledge by self-contained man, who creates an image of God out of his own highest possibilities.

One need not say that this second conversion is therefore less religious than the first. In the first man strives away from himself (as contradictory multiplicity) toward the unity that he is not. In this second one man is self-sufficient and fashions his god according to his own measure. The first way is not, as might superficially be thought, optimistic because it affirms the One as primal light and primal radiation. It posits the One at the cost of the radical denial and dissolution of all worldly reality; it is, therefore, radically pessimistic. The second way, which at first appears pessimistic, because it does not seek to overcome the tension of the opposites, is more deeply affirmative of reality, if only with an heroic emphasis. Thus, it foregoes any other (transcendental) salvation and contents itself with the healing forces which exist in life as it is.

Both ways, however, are seldom found in a pure and separate form; they are generally found combined with either one or the other predominating, but neither wholly absent. Even the mystical ascent to the One demands, in its way, the suffering of a heart that renounces, and the heroic struggle imples ultimately reconciliation. They complement each other, even in their image of god. If the god of the first way is not to be simply an indifferent, heartless void, then emanation has to be understood as "gratutiously self-radiating goodness". If the tragic struggle is to have a divinely significant basis, then the fact that the gods are subject to destiny reveals a vulnerability, a knowledge of their own responsibility, a sharing of the divine ground of things in the fate of the universe.

The world of myth is rich in concepts which foreshadow the true relation of God and the world, in which the elements are mixed and set off against one another in an almost infinite number of ways. Whatever the mixture, whatever images may be used to convey it—from the most primitive African, American Indian, and Polynesian legends to the subtly poised Gnostic myth—the ingredients always yield significant, symbolically profound pictures, which there is no need to classify here. Mythical religions always combined these elements: a sphere of earthly justice, which embraces both the private and the public spheres, in which a provisional ethical catharsis is attempted through renunciation, discipline, suffering, and expiatory, reconciliatory sacrifice. But this is always projected on to a transcendent horizon of heavenly grace, of the promise of salvation on the basis of a covenant relationship to a merciful god, so that the ethico-political order of the earth with its active virtue is made possible by a transcendental relationship to a believed, hoped-for, and (in the loyalty to the god promising it) loved salvation.

Nevertheless, the idea of its emergence on the historical plane—of salvation there from the entanglement of existence—is intensely envisioned, but remains only a vision (a god whose reality is more than mythical is to be found nowhere in history). Hence, the salvation which depends on this contact with the real, mortal world remains always a potential unfulfilled idea. The more spontaneous the influence of the mythical image in the world, the more the earthly order—of peoples and of persons—can be shaped, by it. But with the coming of the age of philosophy, the mythical, magical power of religious images declines, and then the naked helplessness of historical, contradictory man becomes again apparent. Into this situation comes the third way of the Bible and of Christ.

Before we proceed to consider this third way, it is to be noted that the transcendence of human existence, which expresses itself in the search for wholeness in conceptions which are irreconcilable ideas, is an essential law of its being. It is more than an "ideological superstructure" above that which is ultimately fragmentary; it is the movement of the fragment towards its whole. This transcendence expresses itself in the consciousness of the "immortality of the soul", which is the best available expression for the ontological postulate of totality. Inasmuch as "soul" means the "very heart of man's being" which cannot be destroyed by the fact of time's existing in extension, a philosophical insight is expressed here which can be arrived at by man himself and is not achieved only with the Christian revelation. Only this insight itself points to the void, because "immortality of the soul" does not suffice to guarantee an assumption of time into the eternal, which is unthinkable if one makes man the starting point. The mythical imagination must here make up what is missing and what cannot be provided by philosophy. No rational speculation—e.g., concerning the univerzalization of the soul separated from the single body by its relation to the total cosmic material—can offer sufficient foundation on which to base a view of the wholeness of the human fragment. Here lies the grain of truth in the refusal of Karl Barth to accept the "immortality of the soul" as a demonstrable truth. If it can be proved philosophically, it only contains once more a fragmentary answer to the question of the wholeness of man, which receives its full answer only through the way of revelation.

## The Third Way of Love

*Similarities and Differences.* The biblical Christian way could appear, to the superficial gaze, as one of the many variants of the myth, which combines in a particularly happy way the poles of the first and second ways. From the first way it apparently borrows the formal framework of the world's going out from God and returning to God, and according to this structure interprets Christianity by Alexandrian theology (the influence of which continues into Scholasticism and the Renaissance). God the Father is absolute unity; the Son is the potential multiplicity of the world of ideas and the point where the subsequent incarnation takes place; the Holy Ghost is the gatherer of the many, through the ideas, back to the absolutely One. The creation of man and the incarnation of God then appear mainly as the "self-exteriorization" of God, a conceded stooping of the higher to the lower. The ways of the return are mainly those of seeing through multiplicity to its divine ground of unity.

From the second way, however, the Christian one apparently borrows the importance of the painful struggle, which places the cross in the centre, as the reconciliation of the world through pain and as the superheroic fight of the "Lion of Judah" with the powers of chaos and of hell. Through the cross the contradiction of sin is overcome through the contradiction of expiation whereby, as in myth, the cathartic sufferings of the crucified man are placed within the realm of the divine. By the cross the "sufferings of God" reveal to the world his involvement in the fate of his creation. Christianity can be interpreted according to this basic structure, just as convincingly as the Alexandrians understood it according to the first one: e.g., by Luther, Pascal, Böhme, and Baader.

The decisive difference, however, has still not been mentioned: namely, that the salvation event, by means of which man achieves a redemptive relationship to God, occurs in history, that God does not set a sign or speak a word to man, but uses man in all his existential doubtfulness and fragility and imperfectibility as the language in which he expresses the world of redemptive wholeness. God, therefore, uses existence extended in time as the script in which to write for man and the world the sign of a supratemporal eternity. Hence, the man Jesus, whose existence is this sign and word of God to the world, had to live out simultaneously the temporal, tragic separting distance and its conquest through (Augustinian) elective obedience to the choosing will of the Eternal Father, in order to realize mysteriously the essentially irrefrangible wholeness within the essentially uncompletable fragmentary. The question of how that is possible and what form such a life takes will be discussed in the last part of the book. So much is clear, however, at this stage, that if this has happened, historical existence, without being devalued by being regarded as mere appearance and without one's having to turn his back on it, has been put in the movement of returning to God.

The christological synthesis here achieved is fundamentally different from any synthesis of the mythical imagination; its force and effectiveness lay—beyond all expectation and imagination—in the resurrection of the dead. Since Christian teaching from the beginning concentrated on this one point and interpreted everything else—the incarnation, life, teaching, sufferings and ascension of Christ, along with Pentecost—strictly according to this central doctrine, it must be understood as the core of the kerygma. It is impossible to elaborate here on all the illuminating truths which this central idea gathers up and radiates out again. For our subject it is sufficient to note that Christianity, with its declaration of the resurrection of the dead, claims to offer the only complete and satisfying solution of the anthropological problem, and thus to be superior to all the religions and philosophies of the world—only, of course, if it is not understood as a superreligion or a superphilosophy, but as a pure act of God's grace. That the fragmentary ways of thinking found in the humanistic religions—the mystic and the mythical, the monistic and the dualistic—have their value at the level at which they were conceived, has already been suggested. But none were able to place the finitude and temporality of historical man in the lap of God's eternity. This was only possible through Christ's resurrection from the dead.

It remains a mystery which, though inexplicable, is proclaimed as experienced by witness in the middle of history and is accepted in its continuing inexplicability, and yet is seen at the same time as the only valid solution of the mystery of man. So much so, that even if one were to feel impelled to reject the reality of the event as too extravagant, one could still see its possibility and its value as the adequate answer to the question of existence. The Resurrection is not a fairy-tale postscript to the life of Jesus, but is its obvious conclusion and sum. This sum is not, as with other men, at the most a living legacy, a "spirit" which continues to have an influence through time; the "spirit", in the case of this man, is so much alive that it testifies to his total mental-physical reality being alive and present. In the "memory" of his death, as the community of the faithful celebrate it, he is always among them as he who lives forever.

One might consider for a moment what Christian teaching (giving reasons for it as well as drawing conclusions from it) sees together with this fact: that this crucified and resurrected man is in a special sense God's Son. Anthropologically, what distinguishes him from all the mystical sons of God is more important: namely, that he is, in an historical sense, the "Son of Man", a man who was really born and really died, a man who like all men, lived and suffered and then rescued this finite reality of flesh and blood for eternal life, opening up for all his brothers the way out through the portals of Hades. Thus, the first contradiction is overcome: namely, that man is at once nature and spirit, and that the claim of spirit bursts the bounds of nature without being able to do without it. In Christ eternal love and loyalty become possible, without the laws of the physical and mortal heart condemning this love as imagination and as falsehood.

*The Revaluation of Death.* Now we can see that, in order to remove the second and profounder contradiction, the death of this resurrected man had to be revalued and seen as a voluntary death out of love. Through his death the corruption of all hearts—their sinful incapacity for love—is overcome, because it is expiated, borne away, and freed from the paralyzing pressure of fate. We can understand that such an historical existence could only be lived if the human heart, awakened to the fullness of love, was from the beginning enfolded within the heart of God who, by involving himself lovingly in human destiny, sought to overcome that destiny by suffering its conflicts through to their very root. It is not the absolute heroism of a human heart alone which through the conquest of existing fate gives birth to the God (in Rilke's sense) in whom temporal and mortal men are ultimately enfolded and redeemed. Such purely "intransitive love", which by its sheer intensity warms the coldest cosmic nights, had to be divine in the first place in order to be able to perform this work.

However intransitively the love of the man on the cross, abandoned by God, experienced itself—Rilke has here found something which was lost and is nearer to Christianity than he ever thought—it streams directly into the boundlessness of divine love and is a full and complete answer to it. Out of the abyss of total futility and abandonment this love corresponds to the absolute gratuitousness of God's love for the world, which ultimately can find no other argument for itself than itself. Futility and abandonment as the mode of being in the guilt of disobedience become the articulation of the word of faithfulness and innocence; in death itself they have attained the superdeath, the state of being on the other side, within the sheltering womb of eternity. The predatory gesture of voracious death is overcome by the gesture of surrender of the dying man. And this too has its measure in the self-giving of God to the world out of love.

Now at last the aspirations of mysticism and of myth can be fulfilled by there being a true "appearance" of God as the salvation for man. As he pursues the way of salvation, he makes the world transparent for the divine to "appear" through it. This appearing is now no longer a turning away from bleak historical reality—as mystic negation of finitude or as its mythical translation into images of the imagination—no, reality is the place and the material within which the living God appears. In the identity of the Son of Man with the Son of God, not only must the truth of man appear at the same time as the truth of God, but man's love for God must also become identical with the love of God for man. Thus, necessarily, the love of man for man (if it is love which comes up to the Christian standard) must become identical with the love of man for God. It must also be evident that in the tragic, expiatory suffering and death of the one man who at once was man and God, God himself goes into death. He places himself in humble and humbled love in the power of the fate which rules the human world, so that he might be henceforth no longer just the fulfilment of the first divine image of transcendent unity but also the fulfilment of the second, in which the gods as well are drawn into the tragic struggle. But the unity of both images is not to be found in merely seeing them superimposed on each other. This unity is to be discovered in something unexpected, something unrealizable by man on his own, something granted him only as the free self-revelation of the innermost heart of God: that the spirit of God is above all conflict and all fate at precisely that point at which his heart, in the ultimate humility and defencelessness of love, is able to be above all blasphemous attacks, all conflicts, all hate.

*The Old Testament's Idea of Man.* The Old Testament is the preparation for this wholeness. In the history of Israel God not only performs "mighty deeds" for his chosen people and thus shows himself as the true God as against the impotent gods of other peoples, but takes his historical covenant seriously and, when the bride entrusted to him breaks the covenant and behaves like a harlot (Ezek. 16:23), reacts like a deceived and outraged lover. As Lord he must threaten punishment and judgement, but as a lover he cannot help showing the "weakness of love" almost to the point of self-degradation, promising not to leave the truant where she is, but to bring her back and redeem her forever in a new and eternal covenant. In the face of this revelation of the loving heart of God in making this covenant, man is able to ponder his incomprehensible paralysis of heart, his involvement in an immemorial guilt, and to make it intelligible as an ancient falling away from an original covenanted love, which is the only reason for the existence of creatures at all in the reality of the world. The primal legend of Paradise, of original sin and of the punishment of subjection to the powers of death and pain, and of enslavement by the anguish of living may be clothed partly in mythical elements. But it is the expression of that existential difference between the heights of the demands of love and the impossibility of satisfying them which man carries round with him always as a dark mystery, whose reality as "original sin", however, becomes intelligible in the face of the fulfilling of the covenant by the other partner, God.

Reflection on the reality of the covenant which constitutes the history of Israel with God, deepens two truths from century to century, truths which reflect each other and reveal ever further depths. The first truth is that the heart of man fails before God, not just occasionally and by chance, but, if dependent on itself alone, by its very nature. The second is that the heart of God never, under any circumstances, fails man, not only in single events, but always on the basis of his inner necessity to love and his free love involvement with the chosen lover. Therefore God can inspire in the man who fails him the power of love to remain *faithful.*

*The Trinity and the Holy Spirit.* The presence of the self-revealing God is what illuminates man's inadequacy for him; that is why it is impossible for him to take himself just as he finds himself, in his glaring contradictions, as the measure of his self-appraisal. If he attempts it, he can get as far as establishing the existence of this conflict—between the "sensual" and the "suprasensual" man (whom Kant calls the *homo noumenon*). Perhaps he can even identify the "radical evil", which prevents the assimilation of the former to the latter, because the requisite freedom to do this is paralysed. The suprasensual man formulates a resounding categorical imperative, which does not promise the absolute happiness of man if it is obeyed but, in order to be comprehensible, postulates the (unverifiable) idea of man's wholeness, of his freedom and immortality with God. That is as far as the philosophical man can get; but that does not solve the anthropological question. It is only posed in its most acute form. Viewed from it, man is incapable of being whole and, at a more profound level, because of "radical evil" he constitutes a refusal even to start moving towards such unattainable wholeness.

But now this "negative" philosophy is take up into the "positive" philosophy of revelation; man is no longer interpreted within the area of his own mystery. He is to be understood within the space prepared by God's love, in which he is already affected by love: trained by it, directed toward it, freed and fated for it. In this discovery the mystery of the Son of God and of Man is freshly illumined. For if this Son were not orientated toward something above him, then he would not have been man and he would have no followers. If, however, like the others in their inadequacy he had been orientated toward an ideal of himself, then he could not be the redeemer from inadequacy. Here the inner nature of God is revealed to us. What, in self-alienated man, must be a looking upward to God, must be prayer, obedience, faith, hope, and love, in the self-collected Son appears as something absolutely ultimate, something which corresponds to the depths of God. Within God himself there is the original of that of which man's relationship to God is a copy: room for love between Father and Son—for God in the mode of creative giving and for God in the mode of created receiving and giving back in full measure—in the unity of the Spirit of love which alone emerges from the double fount of love and, as the eternal fruit of love, unites and distinguishes the Father and the Son. These unplumable depths of the springs of life in the eternal God are seen as the only sufficient condition for the historical appearance of the Son of God and of Man, since he, appearing in the middle, points behind and above himself to the Father who sent him and promises the Spirit which is freely given to the world and is easily known by it when the "life of the flesh" that leads to death ends, and the "life of the spirit" that resurrects from death begins.

That the Holy Spirit has become freely available to man means that the existence of the Saviour, who resolved the conflict of life and liberated men finally from the power of fate, is not suspended as a purely transcendental idea above the man who follows him. He need not despair of the attainment of the idea in the same way that he was torn apart by the discrepancy between the claims of love and the incapacity of loving. That would be the case of the relationship between the sinner, who contributes nothing to his salvation, and the Saviour, who in place of the sinner obtains and prepares all that is asked of the latter, as if this situation were the last word. If it were, it would still remain an "as if" situation, a purely external accounting of the merits of the Son of God to the meritless sinner, hence a relationship which would not overcome the tragic discrepancy in man himself. If that were the doctrine of radically Protestantism, then it would lack the dimension of the Holy Spirit.

The sending of the Spirit after the completion of the Son's deed of redemption is, again, something quite new: the unique historical deed becoming interior to the narrow, finite consciousness of man. It is force, pressing up from inside man's deepest depths, encouraging him, and empowering him to enter on the venture of Christian love. The Spirit poured out into the hearts of men, of which Paul speaks, and the drastic language of the Church's teaching of the "infused virtues", i.e., strengthening, of faith, hope, and charity, show that the tragic discrepancy in man is led by God the Spirit himself to final annihiliation. This tremendous exertion of man in the Holy Spirit—of the individual and of all men—and with the microcosm of the macrocosm assigned to him, Paul describes in Romans 8 (and John in Revelation 12), with the image of the birth pangs. According to Paul the Holy Spirit of God not only shares in bringing into being the new man and the new world, but his sighs and groans are the real driving force which imperatively demands the impossible of man and through its divine strength achieves it.

Man's way to unity with God is now no longer separate from the way of the man with the bleeding heart. His heart broke on the cross and poured itself out for all men. His Spirit daily opens up that heart and pours from it into all who give themselves over to his guidance. In Christianity man is neither dominated by God (as in the way of union)—he is taken seriously in his difference from God, to the point of God's becoming man himself—nor is he absolutized in his tragic difference by becoming the "battleground of the gods", because the divine Spirit becomes part of him and enfolds his discrepancies (perfecting, preserving them) in the loving differences within God himself. What vastness there is here, what great seriousness of love God reveals when he lets the tragic and apocalyptic differences between God and the world, God and hell, be fully expressed within his own all-embracing differences.

This becomes clear in the first place in the creative work of the Father. In its whole potential and actual falling away, in its tragedy and fatality it had to be not only answered for, but also carried through and supported, in the heart of the Creator. Otherwise, the creating God himself would acquire demonic character—either of a sublime indifference or of being drawn himself into the workings of fate. A God who, out of his own inviolable beatitude, let his creatures suffer and related these sufferings back to his own glorification, would not stand to his creatures in the relationship of original to copy.

This becomes clear in the second place in the work of reconciliation by God the Son, who does not expiate the sin of the world from the separating distance of the (pharaisaically) "pure". Because he is the pure lover, he unreservedly identifies himself with the guilt and the fate of his fellow men. He does not set beside the tragic discrepancy another untragic one. He takes the tragic one into himself and lives it through to its very ground, but with the longer breath of love, which allows him, out of the darkest, most hellish abandonment by God, to be resurrected to the Father and to the world.

This becomes clear in the third place in the redemptive work of the Holy Spirit, who overcomes the remaining sinful discrepancy in sinners, not with the easy superiority of God, but with the infinite labour of one who goes into the bleakness, the narrowness, and the stupor of finite and fallen consciousness in order to open it, together with him and on his conditions, to infinite love. In this humiliation of love the divine Spirit of love reveals its true being. We can see this from the warnings of Paul not to grieve the Spirit, not to extinguish it (as if it were unspeakably sensitive and a tiny delicate flame which is in danger of going out).

The Spirit obviously does not alienate itself in this redemptive work from its own divine nature, but rather places itself inside the heart of the creature. He who "searches the depths of the Godhead" is he who truly knows and has to do with those ultimate possibilities, which lie in God himself, of creating something which shuts itself off in enmity from God and encloses itself in itself with no way out. These are possibilities which cannot have any Christian significance if seen as the draconian measures of a Marcionist Yahweh and a Blakean Urizen or as the (related) hellfire decrees of the God of Tertullian, Calvin, and Jansenius. They become Christian possibilities only through the doctrine of the Holy Spirit, who in its love is beyond these tragic conflicts.

# 4. The Last Five Stations of the Cross

"According to the teaching of the Apostle Paul, the Christian should pray without ceasing (1 Thess 5.17). We learn from the same Apostle that we must always carry about in our body the dying of Jesus, so that the life of Jesus too may be made manifest in our bodily frame" (2 Cor 4.10f.).—*Constitution on the Sacred Liturgy*, I, 12.

*Tenth Station*

What is shame?
The mystery of the body is but a poor allegory.

What *this* body makes visible
is the twisted shape of hearts,
created for love, chosen for love,
that yet offer every insult unto love,
attempt every abuse of its secret and holy nakedness.

White, scourged limbs stripped of allurement.
Blood risen to the head where all sense of shame is
gathered.

And what is this game with the loincloth?
Will they cover him?
Or will they—it is more likely—tear the cloth away?
It makes little difference.
The whole body shouts shame,
has become the utter shame of mankind;
and nothing can conceal that shame any longer

Look at him or look away—it is all the same.
For there *you* are, my friend.
That is how you *really* look.

*Eleventh Station*

Let it happen, Mother.
You cannot change it.
He is older than you are,
and you would not exist
had it not been ordained thus from the beginning.
You stand because he is lying down,
you move freely because he is being nailed to the
cross . . .

This is not your will,
not even your most intensely heroic will:
it is the will of your son, your God,
who is letting himself be crucified for your sake
and for the sake of all men.
Let it happen!
In the name of God, say *yes*!
Deliver your own will unto this alien one
(which grew out of your own
and leads you where you do not want to go).

Say *yes*;
and you will be saved from yourself;
will become the mother of all who say yes;
will be closest of all to him;
and will protect all of mankind under your black
mantle,
Mother of Mercy.

*Twelfth Station*

The man who embraces the cross is always alone,
looking up at one who is not looking down,
but who is in turn looking upward
towards the God who has forsaken them.
That is the important thing:
that he lifts our abandonment into his own greater
abandonment.

Those words he spoke—
that the Father should forgive them;
that his soul is commended to God;
that another will share paradise with him;
that his mother is our mother;
that he thirsts;
that, truly, it has all been done—
having meaning only because he knows what
abandonment is.

"The many" stand around;
some with magnificent gesture,

some alert, waiting, speculating,
all sensing that something may happen yet which concerns them . . .
Because there *is* one unanswered question here:
Is God ultimately revealed?

If yes,
it must be God's *love*
which makes him cry out with us to the One who has vanished,

"*But why?*"
"Why have you forsaken me?"

Let that be God's question to you.

*Thirteenth Station*

The builder is beginning his task.
Standing on the scaffold he busies himself with his tools,
fancying he is an architect,
and builder of a better world.
Fancying too that God desperately needs his help.

Let man think no further.
Leave him to constructive illusions.
Otherwise who could explain this station of the cross?

The bloodless body, free of nails, glides downward.
Someone below supports its weight.
Gently, easily, it sinks,
matter seeking its points of specific gravity.

Is God then far below and not far above?
Are we building high into a void,
into the void of our spirit? . . .

And, almost unaware, releasing God
from our cramping clutch,
leaving him to his own sinking motion? . . .

Rising Eros has its reasons;
this falling Love is its own ground and underground;
sinking out of itself into itself,
past ascending man;
inviting him to surrender all his ground to that
groundlessness
and to rest in the unique Centre.

*Fourteenth Station*

This is what is known as a first-class funeral.
The solicitous ones seem to be chiefly intellectuals.
With solemn gestures they flourish gravecloths,
making a liturgy,
absorbing themselves in its dignity.
Nothing indicates they expect a resurrection.

The corpse is swathed according to custom.
Only the face cannot be subdued.
All suffering stares from that head.
Impossible to wrap it
in a great and festive forgetting.

So already his unquiet image haunts heads and
    hearts.
Already the spirit is freed.
Already the Easter question takes shape . . .

But silently.
For tomorrow is only Holy Saturday.

The day when God is dead,
and the Church holds her breath.
The strange day that separates life and death
in order to join them in a marriage beyond all human
thought.
The day which leads through hell,
and, after all the paths of the world,
into a pathless existence.